GOD'S JUSTICE AND JUDGMENT

A Biblical Insight About God's Justice
and the Protocol of God as the Great King and Judge

W. A. TYRRELL

God's Justice and Judgment
A biblical insight about God's justice and the protocol of God as the great King and Judge.

Copyright 2019 by Wynette A. Tyrrell

ISBN 978-1-947741-42-3

Published by Kingdom Publishing, LLC
1350 Blair Drive, Odenton, MD 21113

Printed in the USA

All rights reserved. No part of this book may be reproduced, stored in retrieval system, or transmitted in any form or by any means - electronic, mechanical, photocopy, recording, or otherwise - except for brief quotations in printed reviews, without the prior written permission of the author.

Unless otherwise indicated, all Scripture quotations are taken from the King James Version (public domain).

Cover Image:
Contributor: RubberBall / Alamy Stock Photo - Image ID: BJG08T

DEDICATION

Thanks be to God the Creator and Judge of the Universe, my Lord and Savior Jesus Christ, who is my Advocate and Redeemer. And special thank you to the Holy Spirit who has guided me and has given me the wisdom and knowledge to write this book. This book is significant evidence that the Lord is a God of Justice and Judgment to all.

God's Justice and Judgment
*A Biblical Insight About God's Justice
and the Protocol of God as the Great King and Judge*

TABLE OF CONTENT

Introduction
The God of Judgment and Justice
1

Chapter 1
The Laws Matter
5

Chapter 2
The Lord our Judge
15

Chapter 3
The Lawgiver
35

Chapter 4
The God of Justice
51

Chapter 5
The Will of God
65

Chapter 6
Our Deliverer and King
75

Chapter 7
His Authority
87

Chapter 8
His Passion for Life
99

Chapter 9
The Captain of Hosts
115

Chapter 10
God is Intentional
123

Chapter 11
A Time for Deliverance
133

Chapter 12
The Blessings of God
143

INTRODUCTION
The God of Justice and Judgment

If the truth be told, there are many people that overlook the very important fact of the judgmental nature of God. Superficially, there are those who think that God is the Father in heaven and His primary function is the attributes of mercy and grace to all mankind. There is a tendency to exclude the fact that one of God's attributes is that of Him being the "Righteous Judge." It is accurate to say that He is the "Only True and Wise God."

> *Our God is in Heaven: He had done whatsoever He had pleased.*
> *(Psalm 115:3)*

> *And the Lord shall be king over the earth: in that day shall there be one Lord, and his name is one.*
> *(Zachariah 14:9)*

The phrase above goes on to say that God sits in the heaven on His throne as the King and Judge and He is doing whatever He desires. This explanation can also mean that the Lord operates in a diversity of ways. The bible is very explicit of God's capacity to function with His legal authority. He is the Creator of all the nations of the world, and He is the judge of all His creation. In other instances, His character reveals that He is the supreme Lawgiver of the world. Likewise, He is referred to as the Lawyer and the Mediator for the children of God.

From a throne room prospective, this was shown throughout the bible stories that the Lord God has a permanent and authoritative position.

We read in the bible, "God is not a man, that He should lie, neither the son of man, that He should repent" (Numbers 23:19). The word of God will stand forever and the Lord our God has the authority to command justice in every area of your life. He has the power to have mercy and compassion. He is the only Advocate, and He has the proficiency to represent and to sanction every case concerning your life. Throughout the history of the prophets of God, they truly revealed the depiction of God as an impartial Judge.

The revelations in this book are designed for you to explore the protocol of God as the great King and Judge. It will bring an informative insight from the a biblical prospective of His Justice and Judgments. This assignment to reveal the nature of God was expedited as an extension of my revelation of His love and grace. His authoritative nature is immeasurable and I came to recognize how God functions as the Righteous Judge. Therefore, in this book, my desire to elaborate on these attributes were irresistible.

The topics of the book is great for group discussion. It will explore many different viewpoints of God's justice and judgments, and an overview of His laws. In fact, it might sway you into believing that the Laws of God still has relevance for today. There are significant discussions to propel you to acknowledge that all of creation owes allegiance to their Creator.

I am persuaded that somehow the principles of God's laws do relate to life today. It will show God is Holy and that righteousness and justice is in His nature. Therefore, at the conclusion of this discussion you will simply be persuaded to reconsider the prospective of God's laws. The documented facts show that Jesus quoted and obeyed the laws throughout His ministry. In some instances, He expounded to the people that all things in the scripture was concerning Himself in relations to Moses and the Prophets, and the laws.

You will read in the bible where Jesus Himself said that He, "Did not come to abolish the laws" (Matthew 5:17). In order to fulfil the laws, Jesus Christ shed His blood to remove the curse of the laws from us (Romans 8:1). The laws referred to are from the sinner's prospective (Roman 6:14). Yet, there are many spiritual leaders who will disagree and try to persuade you that the laws are not applicable today.

Chapter 1
THE LAWS MATTERS

Have you ever stopped to consider if there weren't any laws, what the nations would be like?

Well, without laws there will be confusion and destruction and the legal values of a state of peace will not exist. The purpose for the laws is to institute order and protection, and to prevent injustice. You can recognize in the bible that from creation there is a long history, as far as the legacy of oral law goes.

> *The commandment is a lamp; and the law is light;*
> *and reproofs of instructions are the way of life.*
> *(Proverbs 6:23)*

In one of Jesus' teachings, He overtly said to the people, "I did not come to destroy the law, nor the prophets; rather I came to fulfill them." Jesus added that, when we do break the laws and the commandments, we are not fit for the kingdom of heaven (Matthew 5:17-20). This phrase clarifies that we will not be suitable for a kingship position. The laws must be fulfilled in order that the gift of salvation would operate in your life. Salvation causes every believer to accept that the Lord has set the boundaries for your life. The laws are put in place for mankind to gracefully walk in righteousness or true morality (Psalms 19:8).

> *The law of the Lord is perfect, restoring the soul: the testimony of the Lord is sure, making wise the simple. The statues of the Lord are right, rejoicing the heart: the commandment of the Lord is pure, enlightening the eyes.*
> *(Psalms 19:7-8)*

The concept of the laws is introduced more prominently in the book of Exodus. At that time, it was becoming burdensome for Moses, and in order to relieve himself from the responsibility of trying to solve all the problems of the Israelite people, he wisely accepted the advice of his father-in-law, Jethro. Jethro was a title of a general and he was experienced in managerial skills. He suggested that Moses should choose men from among the tribes and appoint them as Judges and Officers to try the many cases. Moses obeys the divine council of the Lord and wrote the introduction of the Laws. Today, these laws are still used for the solutions of civil and domestic matters (Exodus 18).

The difference between a Judge and an Officer is that the Judge is to help to write laws; the Officer is responsible for enforcing the laws. The Lord commanded Moses to teach the Judge that he or she was expected in turn to conduct judgments and justice with true morals of righteousness. The Judge is to execute justice without partiality, in order to separate the oppressed from their oppressors.

The fundamental laws of the Lord were given first to His chosen people; and these principles of morality was His way to encourage them to model a godly character.

There is evidence that God had His laws in place during the days of Adam and Eve. God had given verbal instructions to Adam to ensure that he would continue to live his life in holiness and righteousness. God told Adam how to distinguish a life of His glory and the judgment for the tree of good and evil. Yet, Adam chose to disobey God's commands (Eve was not given those instructions). This is a controversial topic to this day (Genesis 2:16-22).

> *The Lord God commanded the man, saying, "Of every tree of the garden you may freely eat: But the tree of the knowledge of good and evil, you shall not eat of it, for in the day that you eat thereof you shall surely die."*
> *(Genesis 2:16-17)*

After the fall of Adam, there was a judgment, and a spiritual death that resulted in a lack of his communing with the Lord. The bible says that there was a period of silence from the Lord. Then men prevailed in their sin and wickedness, and the Lord judged the earth with a flood. Without God's law there was chaos.

It took ten generations from Noah to Abraham for God to find a friend. The sages say that from inception God wanted a family and Abraham was chosen by the Lord to start His family. He guided Abraham with His oral laws and Abraham obeyed by walking in righteousness (in right standing) with God. This was prior to the written laws that we now have in the bible or the Hebrew Torah. Many generations after Abraham, the Lord God engraved the Law in stones and gave them to Moses for the people.

The Hebrew scholars say that the law was written in stone in reference to the hearts of men; at the time, the Lord wrote the laws on the outside of men for their hearts was likened to stone. Their deliberation relates to the fact that the laws were designed to be a blessing; and it is a way to encourage love for the Lord and for other people.

In the New Testament, the Apostle Paul enlightened Timothy of the reason for the Law. Paul acknowledged that the law is good, if a man uses it lawfully. He specified that the law was not made for the righteous man, but for the lawless and disobedient, and for the ungodly and for sinners (I Timothy 1:7-9).

The apostle Paul quoted the scripture of the prophet Jeremiah when he declared that the Lord will put the laws into their mind and write them in their hearts. Therefore, with your love for the Lord, there is the process of a changed heart for the laws of the Lord (Hebrew 8:10). The Lord had promised to make a new covenant with His people, to ensure a change of their hearts. He writes the laws on the inside of your human heart and it is revealed in your conscience.

Moses taught that true worship was essential for the Jewish people; they were instructed to worship the God of their fathers – Abraham, Isaac and Jacob (or Israel). He admonished them to keep the Lord's commandments and laws, and to teach them to their children, and their children's children for generations to come. The main principal of these instructions means that you must learn the commands of the Lord so you can teach them to the children. Be mindful of the fact that you cannot teach what you do not know.

The Lord is explicit of His position pertaining to your life and future generations. This requirement is an assurance for His blessings throughout the generations. I have read in the Hebrew culture that the following bible verse of the law is rehearsed in the ears of the people and their children day after day. Today the scripture is still rehearsed intentionally to remind them of the foundation of their faith (Deuteronomy 6:4-7):

You shall Love the Lord your God with all your heart, and with all your soul, and with all you might. And these words, which I command you this day, shall be in your heart: And you shall teach them diligently unto your children, and talk of them when you sit in your house, and when you walk by the way, and when you lie down, and when you rise up.
(Deuteronomy 6:4-7)

The fact is there is no problem with the Laws of God. It is the acceptance of the principle of His laws. The prophet Hosea gave a call for the obligation to obey the Lord's commands. He declared that the righteous has no problem with obeying the laws; for in their obedience they receive their reward of mercy.

The bible enunciates that the Lord is a God of judgment and justice. There is an abundance of evidence that shows that the laws and statues of the Lord are conditional even though the Lord is a loving and a compassionate God. Moses and the prophets declared this in the Old Testament. I will be addressing a few of these declarations in detail later. There is a declaration in the book of Proverbs which states that there are things that God *loves* and there are things that God *hates*.

We read, "For God so loved the World, that He gave his only begotten son; that whosoever believe in Him should not perish but have everlasting life" (John 3:16). This declaration tells us of His nature of love. However, this phrase seems debatable when we think of His judgments. God has not lessened His desire for salvation and He does not hate people. To clarify, it is basically that the Lord does hate and disapprove of the things people do that are contrary to His word. His distaste for your disobedience and unbelief is measured in comparison to His laws.

The Freedom to Choose

Who is Wise, and he shall understand these things? Prudent and he shall know them? For the ways of the Lord are right, and the just shall walk in them: but the transgressors shall fall therein.
(Hosea 14:9)

There are times when an unfavorable circumstance occurs and I often wonder why an individual would allege that God is the reason why bad things happen to good people. In these instances, I would reflect to the attributes of God and remind myself that nothing happens by chance because "He is a Righteous God." Some things are unexplainable and it is reasonable to examine the Lord's guideline for the errors. God uses a measuring stick for all His blessings toward mankind (Roman 12:3). His physical law has involved the foundation of righteousness; and the believer is admonished to live an exclusive lifestyle (Deuteronomy 28).

Cursed be the man that make any graven or molten image, it is abomination unto the Lord, the work of the hands of the craftsman, and put it in a secret place.
(Deuteronomy 27:15)

The content of this discussion is designed to shine a light on one of the greatest gifts besides salvation that the Lord has given man – a free-will. Today, you have the freedom to choose. However, there are only two choices. It is either to obey or disobey. The fact is whether you want the truth and the acceptance of the Lord Jesus Christ or where you desire to spend eternity (Luke 13:27). It is entirely up to you to decide. The salvation plan of truth is Jesus Christ. He is the only way to God. The rejection of Jesus leads to unbelief and sin; the consequences of sin is spiritual death and destruction.

There are two groups of people in the world. The first group of people are the men and women who walk in obedience with the Lord and the second group walks in disobedience. There are examples in the bible of obedient people that can be associated with the fathers of faith, i.e. Abraham, Isaac and Jacob. Also, there are those that disobey and their behavior results in rebellion, unbelief, and unfaithfulness against God.

The highlight of all the stories told of the disobedient is that of Lucifer, the archangel of Light. He is also known as Satan, and he chose his pride and rebellion against God. Also, there were some prime characters that operated in disobedience to the Lord such as king Saul who lost his kingship as a result of the sin of pride and disobedience. Then there was king Solomon and he is spoken of as the wisest king. However, his sin of pride was imminent, and it caused the judgment of the Lord to divide the kingdom into two. Many of the kings of Israel and the priests of the Lord's tabernacle were included with those that chose disobedience against the Lord.

I heard a pastor make this following statement: "God chose you and He chose the world, but those that are in heaven are the ones that chose God." It touched my heart and I said, "Lord, help me to choose you every day of my life." I hope this will be your prayer, too.

You can read of one story that I found interesting and its relevance to the freedom to choose. There was a king named Manasseh, who was the son of king Hezekiah. As he grew up his father's sins were known to him and the judgment of God that result in the blessings of his birth. Yet, he chose to be rebellious against the Lord. The story of his dilemma in Babylon and his repentance to choose to return to God was enlightening. It is an example of the mercies of the Lord over His judgment (2 Kings 21).

> *The heart is deceitful above all things, and desperately wicked: who can know it? I the Lord search the heart, I try test the emotions, even to give every man according to his ways, and according to the fruit of his doing.*
> *(Jeremiah 17:9)*

A Judgment Day is Coming!

The bible declares that we will all stand before God to give an account for all we have done in our lifetime. At the mentioning of the word "judgment," you immediately anticipate that there will be death and destruction. Moreover, there will be two judgments on that day; most people never consider this fact. On judgment day, the Lord Jesus Christ will appear in His glorious splendor to receive His own to Himself, and they will reign with Him eternally. Therefore, it will be a day of blessings for the saints and the saved; this experience is known as the rapture.

At the same time, it will be a day of judgment for the sinners, the disobedient and rebellious ones. The book of Revelation says that they will be cast away and rejected from the Lord. Subsequently, they will be given over to the devil, and the wicked will be cast out into an eternal darkness and an unquenchable fire.

The apostle Peter, in his writings, has revealed that in the judgment of the Lord there will be no exceptions for saints or believers. Peter quoted Genesis of God's decision for sin. He stated, "For God did not spare even the angels that had sinned, but He cast them down into hell; and He delivered them into chains of darkness, to be reserved for the judgment day." He continued by explaining, "God did not spare the old world from destruction." Yet, God saved Noah and his family of eight. Noah was a preacher of righteousness, and he was morally right in the sight of God.

In the following verses, Peter explains that God brought the flood upon the earth as a means of destruction in order to judge the ungodly. In addition, he reminded the followers of Jesus Christ that the catastrophic event concerning the cities of Sodom and Gomorrah was one of God's fierce judgment. For the Lord had condemned them with an overthrow and by fire He turned them into ashes. This was done to make the cities an example for those that should live ungodly in the future (2 Peter 2:4-6).

The Lord had made all things for himself: yes, even the wicked for the day of evil.
(Proverbs 16:4)

Jesus' Power Over Sin

We have the ability to do the Will of God with the help of the Holy Spirit. The bible declares that the Lord Jesus has all power over the law of sin and death. He is the Lord of hosts and the God of the angel armies (Joshua 5:14). The Lord has a warrior spirit by nature. He is likened to a Rock. This means that He is durable. As you visualize a rock, you see its quality of longevity and it relates to the divine and eternal lifespan. Therefore, the Lord has the durability to fight your battles. Always and forever, He will command the law of justice on your behalf.

The Passover season is to remind us of the battles Jesus endured and the victory He won for you on Calvary's cross. The bible says, "For the laws of Moses could not deliver us from our weaknesses, but Christ came that the righteousness of the law might be fulfilled in us." Moreover, this phrase details that as a believer, we must walk after the Lord in the Spirit and that we deny the things of the flesh (Romans 8:2-4). God's divine plan was to have fellowship with mankind from the beginning of time, but through the fall we had to be reconciled through Jesus Christ.

Some time ago, I heard a song that says, "He is a God of Faithfulness, without injustice, good and upright is our Lord" (Deuteronomy 32:4). You must learn to embrace the fact that the Lord is still fighting battles for your justice today. Jesus has paid the ransom for your sins by the shedding of His own blood. He has prevailed in victory over all wickedness and sins by His precious blood and His power. The atonement actions of the Lamb of God had made the pathway clear for you to have fellowship with the Lord, and His Father God for all eternity.

> *There is none Holy as the Lord: for there is none besides You: neither is there any rock like our God.*
> *(I Samuel 2:2)*

The Laws Matter

He is the Rock, His works is perfect: for all His ways are judgment: a God of truth and without iniquity, just and right is he.
(Deuteronomy 32:4)

Thy righteousness is an everlasting righteousness, and thy law is the truth.
(Psalm 119:142)

Chapter 2
THE LORD OUR JUDGE

For we must all appear before the judgement seat of Christ; that everyone may receive the things done in his body, according to that he had done, whether good or bad.
(2 Corinthians 5:10)

God is our Creator and He is predominantly a Righteous Judge (Genesis 1:1). Still today, Jesus embraces a lawful position over your life to do justice and judgment unconditionally. His attribute as the Judge means that He has all power and authority to sanction all outcomes. There are many testimonies of His judgments. His judicial office is illuminated by His prophets, and there are many recorded declarations of their experiences with the Lord God. Similarly, the bible has recorded multiple examples of His lovingkindness, His mercy and compassion. (Genesis 2:4).

The bible defines the Lord as "God and the Supreme Judge, who executes justice to the meek, and He reserves the wicked unto the day of judgment to be punished" (Psalm 37:37-40). However, it is accurate to say that most people usually relate to the judgmental personality of the Lord, and this depends on their experiences in their journey in life. In conversations people describe the Lord as the "Supreme Being," mostly voicing their opinion of God having a rigid fist. Other times you would hear conversations of those who imagine that God acts mostly judgmental, with a coldhearted personality.

There are several stories told of the Lord's character as a Judge in the bible. One of the captivating stories was that of His judgment against the King of Judah. The King of Israel came to visit the king of Judah because they were allies. He was wanting to involve the King of Israel into doing battle against their enemy, the King of Syria. It seemed that the King of Israel was hesitant to enter a compulsory war with Judah. He wisely considered and suggested they should inquire of the council of the Lord in this matter. The King of Judah agreed to receive the council of the prophets of Judah; and their advice was for the two kings to engage in a battle with the Syrian king.

Someone must have mentioned it to the prophet Micaiah; for he was absent during the council of the prophets of Judah. His reputation was known for his integrity and truthfulness. The King of Judah hated Micaiah because his prophecies would come to pass every time. This happened all the while the King of Judah reigned. Micaiah would speak whatever the Lord had said regardless if it was good or bad.

The King of Israel requested that the prophet Micaiah should be brought before the kings. It was difficult for the king of Israel to accept Micaiah's council because he had never done so before. In the presence of the people, the prophet Micaiah was commanded to speak whatever the Lord was saying. Micaiah, in his wisdom, initially repeated exactly what all the other prophets had proposed.

However, the kings insisted to know the truth, so the prophet Micaiah changed his story and declared exactly what the Lord had revealed to him. He declared that the judgment of God would prevail over the nation. He said that he saw the people of Israel scattering in defeat. It was at the same moment that the prophet Micaiah prophesied and declared that the Lord God was positioned in the seat upon His throne, in heaven as the Judge; and all the host of heaven was surrounding God liken to a judicial court system. This prophecy of Micaiah confirmed that God is Judge over all the nations.

> *Micaiah the prophet said, Hear therefore the word of the Lord: "I saw the Lord sitting on his throne, and all the host of heaven standing by him on His right hand and on His left.*
> *(1 Kings 22:19)*

Another declaration from the prophet Isaiah specifies that God is the Righteous Judge. He declared that all the nations of the world will desire to come up to the mountain of the Lord; and their hearts will desire to be taught His ways. Then, the nations will inquire to know the God of Jacob in order that they could walk in the paths of righteousness and holiness. Here, Isaiah acknowledges that the 'Laws' and the Word of the Lord shall be preached to the people of the nations in the city of Jerusalem. The prophecy of Isaiah is fulfilled today; for many people are going to Israel, to find the truth. Isaiah declares that the answer to the truth is in Christ Jesus; for He is the light of the world, and His righteousness is the Laws of God (Isaiah 2:3-5). The other prophets make similar declarations of the Godhead nature of Christ the Lord.

> *He is our Judge, the Lord is our Lawgiver, the Lord is our King.*
> *(Isaiah 33:22)*

> *The Captain of Hosts was the way Joshua revealed him.*
> *(Joshua 5:14)*

> *The God of all flesh was Jeremiah's declaration.*
> *(Jeremiah 32:27)*

> *The Lord is our defense and the Holy one.*
> *(Psalm 89:18)*

His Judicial Court

You have read that the Lord God is the Judge and He sits in His judgment seat. It has shown that there is a judicial court system operating in heaven. The prophet Daniel gave an explicit account of a divine protocol of the Judge. The scenery displayed that God is rendering His verdicts, judgments and sentences from His throne. This statement consists of His justice and His divine order in all the earth.

> *I saw in the night vision, and behold, one like the Son of man came with the clouds of heaven, and came to the Ancient of days, and they brought him near before Him. And there was given Him dominion, and glory, and a kingdom that all people, nations, and languages, should serve Him: his dominion is an everlasting dominion, which shall not pass away, and his kingdom that which shall not be destroyer.*
> *(Daniel 7: 13-14)*

The Lord instructed Moses, the servant of God, to set up the judicial pattern upon the earth that was identical to the vision he had seen in heaven. Moses saw that God is seated upon His throne; and the Lord stood as the Mediator in the courtroom (Hebrews 8:5). His declaration is another confirmation that in heaven above, the Lord is seated at the right hand of God, and He intercedes for the accused, or makes intercession for you. Through Jesus Christ's death and resurrection, His blood creates a new covenant for us. Jesus was able to bring Father God and mankind into agreement again. It also means that you and I, who are washed in the precious blood of Jesus Christ, have been delivered from the judgments of God.

Traditional Jews say that the destiny of the righteous and the wicked will be determined on the Lord's Judgment Day; and on that day their names will be written in the Book of Life or in the Book of Death.

> *And whosoever was not found written in the book of life was cast into the lake of fire.*
> *(Revelation 20:15)*

His Judgments

The judgment of God is sure and is according to truth (Romans 2:2). Virtually, all the Lord's judgments come upon people when they are blessed but forget the 'Blesser.' It is usually when we have needs that we turn to Him for help. The apostle Paul had revealed that the wrath of God comes from heaven, and it is against all ungodliness and unrighteousness (Romans 1:18). Therefore, it is truth verses untruth that results in the judgment of the Lord.

God's Justice and Judgment

In God's judgments it is clearly seen that there is a grace and mercy factor. The scene of God's judgment was portrayed in the story of Adam and Eve. God had created Adam first, then He planted a garden for him to dwell in and have authority in. The consequence of Adam's sin caused the Lord to judge him. He was sent out from the place where he communed daily with the Lord. Then, God placed cherubim, with flaming swords, to block man's way from ever entering again into the Garden of Eden.

Most people blame Eve for the sin, however, in revisiting the text, Adam was alone when the Lord gave him the law. Afterwards, He created Eve. It was Adam's error for not teaching his wife the commands that resulted in their expulsion from the Garden of Eden. They were driven out of the garden immediately; it was the lack of conversation that caused the disconnect from intimacy with the Lord. Their sin and unbelief had caused a limited fellowship between God and mankind.

I often wonder why the tree was there in the first place? In a biblical commentary, I found two theories that made some reasonable explanations. They suggested that one of the reasons God left the tree of Good and Evil in the midst of the garden was for Himself. The other purpose was that the tree was to remind Adam and Eve that God was in charge as their Creator.

I found a theory for cherubim with flaming swords outside the garden. The sages say that even though Adam and Eve disobeyed or rebelled against God, nevertheless, in His mercy and grace, He had placed the cherubim at the entrance with the flaming light to show man the way back to God. In fact, the bible never mentioned if Adam and Eve ever repented. Could this be the reason why God's judgment lasted for such awhile? In the history of the Hebrew nation from Moses to their Messiah, Jesus Christ, it took many decades for man to be reconciled back to God.

> *He drove out the man, and He place at the east of the garden of Eden Cherubims, and a flaming sword which turned every way, to keep the way of the tree of life.*
> *(Genesis 3:24)*

The biblical principles state that God is the Righteous Judge of all. He is our Creator and He expects all people to respect Him. He can bring life and death to the world. The bible declares that one day, according to His glorious appearance, He will stand as Lord and King to judge the world. The prophet Zephaniah declared that it will be a day of the Lord's judgment. He calls it a great day; a day of wrath, a day of trouble and distress, a day of suddenness and desolation. It will be a day of warring, of darkness and gloominess (Zephaniah 1:14-16).

In the book of Isaiah, the prophet declares that the Lord is the judge of all, and He shall judge among all the nations and the people. Isaiah says that God, as Lord of Hosts, shall judge the proud and the lofty, and every one that lifts up their head in pride shall be made low (Isaiah 2).

We read in the book of Malachi that the prophet declared, on God's appointed time, the Lord will return as a Refiner's fire, and all will stand before Him to be judged (Malachi 3:1-3). He will return as a refiner's fire seems antagonistic in contrast with the Lord being a merciful God. Though the word fire has many negative analogies, it does consist of some positive ambiances. Fire is a fuel that can be used to give warmth in cool places or it can be used to make inedible things become digestive.

The properties of fire consist of heat that is liken to a burning and consuming action that has the capability for removing impurities. Fire can also be used to cleanse and refine things systematically. Also, fire is known to be used to form shapes and preserve things, for example, steel. These explanations can relate to the power and force in terms of the character of the Lord as a refiner's fire; the Holy Ghost fire through which there would be a purging and cleansing.

The Lord's righteous judgment will entail a cleansing. It will also mean that only those who are washed and cleansed with the precious blood of Jesus will be able to stand before Him.

> *Who may abide in the day of His coming? And who shall stand when He appears? For He is like a refiner's fire, and like a cleanser.*
> *(Malachi 3:2)*

Jeremiah the prophet had a dream and received a revelation of the Lord's word being like fire (Jeremiah 23:29). The Lord reassures Jeremiah of His power. The author of the book of Hebrews declared, *"For the word of God is quick and powerful, and sharper than any two-edged sword piercing even to the dividing asunder of soul and spirit, and of the joints and marrow, and is a discerner of the thoughts and intents of the heart"* (Hebrews 4:12). Subsequently, this means that the word of God can judge even the heart of a man.

Moses had declared that out of the Lord's right hand went a fiery law (Deuteronomy 33:2). We read in the scriptures of Zephaniah that God's jealousy is likened to fire, to judge the kingdoms of the earth (Zephaniah 3:8).

The significance of repentance is vital. The word *repentance* in Hebrew is *"teshuvah"* and it means *"to return."* The word implies a state of disobedience to God's laws; for it is your moral duty and destiny to be with God. Therefore, the implication of repentance is in comparison to the description of God's judgment.

It is absolutely necessary for you to seek the Lord in repentance and to be washed in the blood of Jesus Christ. This will guarantee you a secure relationship with the Lord Jesus Christ and the Holy Spirit. The Holy Spirit is the person that shines the light of the revelation within your heart and to the Lord Jesus, and God's righteous judgment will speak on your behalf, causing you to be reconciled back to God.

Adonai- the Merciful Judge

Adonai is one of the names of God. The Hebrew meaning of the word is "A Merciful Judge" (Exodus 34:6-7).

In His mercy, God used the animal's skin to cover Adam and Eve when He found them in the garden. This was a sign of the first sacrifice of the Lamb of God, and the blood was used for the atonement for their sins. The sages say that this act of covering was a foreshadow of the crucifixion of Jesus Christ. For with His love He has given His life in exchange for your mercy.

In one particular encounter with Moses, the Lord proclaimed Himself to be the "Lord God Almighty." He revealed that He was the supreme ruler over all creation and over all mankind. The Jewish people, out of respect for God, addresses Him as Adonai – a Merciful God. God had also told

Moses that His mercy is reasonable and His judgment is to the third and fourth generation. He is still merciful and forgiving before and after a man commits sin. The Lord's desire was for all the people to delight themselves in Him and to obey the laws of God.

> *Blessed is the man that trust in the Lord, and whose*
> *hope is in the Lord.*
> *(Jeremiah 17:7)*

Moses was instructed to convey God's judgments and His rewards. They will be rewarded blessings for their obedience or judgment for their disobedience. When Moses had finished speaking, the people of Israel made a covenant with the Lord and they responded by saying, "All the judgments, and all the words of the Lord; we will do!" (Exodus 24:3)

The Hebrew scholars say that it was like a marriage ceremony between the Lord and His chosen people at Mount Sinai. They had given their vows and they had verbalized their promise, "I will!" and "I do!" Then, Moses rose up early in the morning and made a memorial of twelve pillars, according to the tribes of Israel. You can read the captivated accounts of what the Lord as a Merciful Judge did for the Israelite people in Psalm 106.

There are other incredible acts of the judgment of the Lord found in the bible. The story of the Pharaoh of Egypt and his encounters with the Lord when he refused to free the Hebrew people from their slavery. It began as Moses was sent from God to speak to the Pharaoh. Every time Moses spoke to him, he became relentless, and he increased the labor for the Hebrew people. Therefore, the Lord executed His justice and judgment on the Pharaoh.

God is very humorous; for in His mercy the fight between Him and the Pharaoh was extended; for God could have ended their dispute in one day. However, the Lord is still a merciful Judge, and with His nature of compassion He strengthened Pharaoh for every bout of plagues. The sages described it like a boxing match, for the Lord had physically intervened on behalf of the children of Israel. He used plagues of gods that they were familiar with. It did not deter the Pharaoh and God had to use the heartbreak of the firstborn sons. The tenth and final blow struck Pharaoh below the belt; this caused a great cry throughout Egypt. Then the Pharaoh let them go, and the Lord delivered His chosen people with His mighty right hand and brought them out of their bondage. The finishing touch of His judgment was the defeat of the Egyptians as the Pharaoh's army were drowned in the bottom of the Red Sea (Exodus 14:27-31).

> *He saved them for His name's sake, that He might make his mighty power to be known. He rebuked the Rea sea also, and it dried up: so, He led them through the depths, as through the wilderness. And He saved them from the hand of him that hated them, and redeemed them from the hand of the enemy. And the water covered their enemies: there was not one of them left.*
> *(Psalm 106:8-11)*

The merciful judgment of the Lord is a controversy in the story of the king Manasseh of Judah. He was the king Hezekiah's son. Manasseh lived in the days of the prophets and during the time of prophet Jeremiah. He was born at a time when his father did good in the sight of the Lord. He would have heard stories of his father's past.

However, king Manasseh's reputation was that he was in his teens when he had become the king, and he refused the council of the prophets. He chose to do evil in the sight of the Lord and rebuilt every high place that his father Hezekiah had broken down. Manasseh erected altars in the house of the Lord where he worshiped Baalim and the zodiac in the heaven. Also, he worshiped the god in the valley of blood by passing his son through the fire as a sacrifice. It got even worse; for the king did every abomination against the Lord. He used enchantments, exercised witchcraft, and observed times; and he dealt with wizards and familiar spirit that provoked the Lord to anger (2 Chronicles 33:1-13). The Lord call his actions worse than the heathen nations.

Nevertheless, God in His mercy gave Manasseh a chance to repent but he refused. Then, the Lord administered His judgment through the king of Assyria, and Manasseh was captured and was bound in chains and carried off to Babylon. After he was afflicted, he cried out to the Lord, the God of his fathers. He humbled himself with prayer, and the Lord heard his prayers and delivered him and brought him back to Jerusalem into his kingdom.

Then king Manasseh recognized that the Lord is God and He is a Merciful Judge; and he turned to God with his whole heart. At that point, he repaired the wall, and broke down the altars. Also, he took away all the strange gods out of the house of the Lord. The bible says that the king prayed to the Lord and he commanded all of Judah to serve the Lord God of Israel for the rest of his reign.

The Sages say that Manasseh's behavior is debatable. According to the laws and the judgment of the Lord, king Manasseh's sins were not supposed to be negotiable. However, based on his true repentance of his sins, he was justified and reconciled to God. This story has portrayed the very nature of a loving God and it shows the mercy and compassion that the Lord has towards the repentant heart.

Moses' Final Speech

On the day that Moses was celebrating his one hundred and twentieth birthday, he assembled all the elders and the Hebrew people in the wilderness, and began to rehearse the mercies and the judgment of the Lord. He cautioned the people of how the Lord's mercies are conditional, and His mercy will not always work to their advantage. Moses voiced his concern because they had yet to reach the promised land – mainly because of their disobedience and rebellion. He felt their incessant, sinful attitude towards the Lord would cause them to experience great judgment after he was gone.

In addition, Moses foretold of the consequences of God's judgment against acts of disobedience. Subsequent to the death of Moses, the people still despised the Lord's commands and God became angry. Just as Moses had prophesied when they crossed over into the promised land, the Lord appointed terror and judgments over them. In His Judgment, He rooted them out and scattered them among the other nations. They began to experience the plagues of the Egyptians and the death of their sons and their daughters.

> *"I know after my death you will absolutely corrupt yourselves, and turn aside from the way which I have commanded you; and evil will befall you in the latter days; because you will do evil in the sight of the Lord,*

> *to provoke Him to anger through the works of your hands."*
> *(Deuteronomy 31:29)*

When we read the bible and see all things that the Lord had done to the children of disobedience, could it be that His judgments are relevant today?

The conditions and the many circumstances pertaining to the judgments of God are listed in the book of Leviticus (Chapter 25). In my circumstances, I envision that His judgment is in relation to each act of my disobedience. This is something to consider with each action you take.

Look at each society in the world today and the extensive epidemic of violence and rioting. According to historical reports, disasters have increased over the past few years. The regular occurrence of storms and hurricanes, and the devastation of the earthquakes, does show signs of something unexplainable naturally. It is also disturbing to hear of the frequent gunning down of innocent young people without probable cause. It makes you question where the laws play a part in the lives of those involved.

It seems like the plague of Ebola and pestilence like Zika are invading the world. All these things seem like the plagues of Egypt. The many circumstances that are surrounded with sadness and death seem concerning. The bible declares that God had promised consequences to the children of disobedience. I pray for the mercy of Adonai over your life today.

> *Who is wise? Let them realize these things. Who is discerning? Let them understand. The ways of the LORD are right; the righteous walk in them.*
> *(Hosea 14:9)*

The Laws of Priestly Role

Jesus is our High Priest and He is still our Judge in this capacity. According to the commands of God, the High Priests had the responsibility of the Judge. The Jewish Judges and priests were different from the rulers of other nations. They had to perform the diagnostic decree of a doctor; they practically were the examiners and the pronouncers of anyone that was diseased with a plague. It was the priest's sanction that caused a person to be deemed clean or unclean. The Lord had given the instruction of how much time the one infected should be separated from the among the others (Leviticus 27).

They were responsible for the temple sacrifices and attending to the upkeep of the house of the Lord. They were to keep the fire burning and candles always lit. They had to ensure that the bread was freshly baked and available each day. They were to attend to the altar and had to sprinkle the blood of the Lamb on appointed occasions in the Holy Place. The sages say that all these duties were a foreshadow of the coming Messiah, Jesus Christ. For Jesus is the bread of life, the light of the world and the sacrificial lamb whose blood was shed for all.

Moreover, the priests had to act as a proxy Judge for the Lord, and in more than one capacity. They were not above the laws of God, but they had the authority of the Judges and the Lawyers for all situations amongst the tribes. Their responsibilities involved making decisions in the nation's civil and domestic laws. The priests would act as part of the counselor of the religious controversy in their nation. For example, it was their duty to judge every civil case that involved a legal dispute between two or more people. The priests were prohibited to take bribes or to justify one person over another.

The High priest also had a very significant assignment from the Lord. He was commanded to pray and pronounce the "Priestly Blessings" over the people. This blessing is done when the people are assembled at the tabernacle. The significance of the blessing was a depiction and a symbol that the Lord wants to put His name and His blessings on His people. The Jews understand this phase to mean that the Lord God wants to place His righteous judgment upon you. This custom is still practiced today, as the Rabbi raises his hands and recites this priestly blessing.

> *The Lord Bless you, and keep you: The Lord make His face shine upon you, and be gracious unto you: The Lord lift up His countenance upon thee, and give you Peace.*
> *(Numbers 6:24:27)*

God's Standards

There is a godly standard that is mandatory for the priestly office; it is termed higher than that of the ordinary men. The High Priest was expected to be one of a 'Righteous' character and his demeanor should be of a distinctive character that portrays that he is chosen of the Lord. He was prohibited to use any strong drink in his service to the Lord. This trait is a symbol of separation from the usual practices of a worldly man. These commands were directly given from the Lord. The laws of the anointed Priest are mainly specified in the book of Leviticus.

In the New Testament, the same reference of the Lord's command was given to John the Baptist's parents. The angel of God commissioned John not to use any strong drink in his walk with God. The priests were required to walk in unity and without unrighteousness.

> *For He shall be great in the sight of the Lord, and shall drink neither wine nor strong drinks; and he shall be filled with the Holy Ghost, even from his mother's womb.*
> (Luke 1:13-14)

It was required for the priest to be cleansed before he could conduct the sacrifices in the Holy Place. The tabernacle of the Lord is proclaimed to be a holy place. Therefore, in God's standards, at the disobedience of His commands, Aaron the High Priest sons', Nadab and Abihu, were judged by the Lord in an instant with death. Subsequently, Moses had just offered sacrifice to the Lord, and the sons of Aaron and the people had just seen the manifestation of the Lord liken to a consuming fire.

This incident of the judgments of God over Aaron's sons was after they saw the fire of God, and Nadab and Abihu still decided to offer *'strange fire,'* on the altar, and they fell dead (Leviticus 10).

There are different commentaries of the Hebrew scholars that give the reasons for the judgment of the sons of Aaron. One says that perhaps Aaron's sons might have been drunk at the time and as they approached the altar, the glory of the Lord stroke them down. This comment teaches the believer in Jesus Christ that it is necessary to be mindful of the condition and character in presenting and representing the Lord.

Another theory states that the sons of Aaron must have entered the Holy of Holies at a time that they were not allowed to. According to Jewish tradition, the priest could only enter the Holy Place at specific seasons and times. Yom Kippur or the Day of Atonement is one of the days appointed for the priest to enter the holiest place. This is known as the holiest day. Every atonement made was the foreshadow of the Lamb of God. Jesus our High Priest entered with His blood and made the atonement for our sins. These specific times are called the Lord's Feast Days, and it is a time when He wants to meet with His people (Leviticus 23).

> *And the Lord spoke to Aaron, saying, "Do not drink wine nor strong drink. You, nor your sons with you, when you go into the tabernacle of the congregation, lest you die: it shall be a statue forever throughout your generations."*
> *(Leviticus 10:9)*

> *The Lord spoke to Moses saying, Speak to the children of Israel, concerning the feasts of the Lord, which you shall proclaim to be holy convocations, even these are my meetings.*
> *(Leviticus 23:1-43)*

The people were dishonorable to the Lordship of God, and they were ungrateful for all that He had done for them. The prophet, Malachi, was around when the children of God continually behaved unthankful to the Lord. In those days, even the priest had begun disrespecting the Lord after Israel came into the land of Promise. Malachi began to rebuke the people; his prophetic utterances were that of God promising to send curses upon the people if they did not worship Him with a right heart (Malachi 1:6-14). The Lord had accused the priest of offering half-hearted sacrifices and polluted bread upon His altar.

    The sages say that the people were stealing the sacrifices that they brought for offerings. The Lord called these offerings blind and lame, torn and sick sacrifices. In His anger, the Lord questioned if the priest and the people would consider giving such offerings to their governors or their kings. They would have more respect for these officials, because they would fear for their lives. The notion of the offering is a valid fact, even in your life today. The body of Christ never think that the Lord can be troubled by our gifts. Even more so, He will be concerned with the aspect of your offering of kindness and compassion to others.

> *A son honors his father, and a servant his master: if then I be a Father, where is my honor? And if I be a master, where is my fear? saith the Lord of hosts unto you, O priests, that despise my name. And you say, Where in have we despise your name?*
> *(Malachi 1:6)*

Chapter 3
THE LAWGIVER

As for me, this is my covenant says the Lord; My spirit that is upon you, and my words which I have put in your mouth shall not depart out of your mouth; nor out of the mouth of your seed, nor out of the mouth of your seed's seed, said the Lord, from henceforth and forever.
(Isaiah 59:21)

I was captivated with the book of Leviticus; it seems to be one of the most intensive law books. These laws seem diverse, yet it is unified to reflect a theme of holiness to the Lord. The concept of the term "Law" is that of a legal principle. These laws can permeate our lives; in addition, the detailed regulations are there to address specific issues. The Lord has guidelines for the personal and communal lifestyle of His chosen people. He categorically made practical laws for Moses to teach the people concerning a healthy wellbeing (Leviticus 11).

The laws and statutes of God are explicit in the scriptures. God has created us with His laws in our hearts. This can truly explain our conscience, which can differentiate between the actions of right and wrong. The word of God accentuates that the Lord will give His people a new heart and a new spirit. This phrase could be interpreted as, 'He will write His laws upon your heart, and He will put His spirit within you, to enable you to keep His laws' (Isaiah 59:21). The Lord has promised the supernatural working in you. It will cause you to trust in Him and to no longer be offensive to His word.

A new heart also will I give you, and a new spirit will I put within you: and I will take away the stony heart out of your flesh, and I will give you a heart of flesh.
(Ezekiel 36:26)

There is one Lawgiver, who is able to save and to destroy.
(James 4:12)

Laws for the King

There is the law regarding a King. The Lord gave to Moses commands long before there was ever a king in Israel. He had detailed the expectation of the position and character of a king. The King is required to rewrite a copy of the laws out of the original book for himself according to the Lord. He is supposed to learn to fear the Lord and to keep all the words of the law and statutes. The King is expected to honor God and practice the written laws of dos and don'ts (Deuteronomy 17:14- 20). The chronicles of king Saul and Solomon showed that they had displayed the opposite of God's command.

Noah Knew the Law

Let us revisit Noah. In ancient times before the flood occurred, Noah and the people were vegetarians. After the flood, God told Noah he could eat meat, if he so desired. On this occasion when Noah and his family had entered the ark, he brought all varieties of animals on board and of each kind Noah carried seven clean and one unclean. Apparently, Noah had insight of the concept of what was the abominable things. The bible says when Noah went out of the Ark afterwards, he built an altar and offered the sacrifice of the clean animals to the Lord. This is an indication that God's oral laws were available in the days of Noah.

> *Noah build an altar unto the Lord; and took of every clean beast, and of every clean fowl, and offered burnt offering on the altar.*
> *(Genesis 8:20)*

The Hebrew Laws

The Lord had designed many other laws you can explore in the word of God. The Hebrew scholars say that there are over six hundred and thirteen (613) laws or commandments written in the bible.

These commands basically are very useful keys for wisdom and good health – in relation to your wellbeing. Yet, only Jesus Christ and the Holy Spirit can help us to obey whatever is required for living a blessed life. I find reading the laws very edifying, and a few interesting 'Laws' I came across I will share that the Lord designed with such precision and gave them to Moses and the people. These are the laws:

- Health Laws
  - *A Law for women and pregnancy.*

- The Law for sicknesses.
- The Protection Laws
  - The Laws for Intentional Sins and Unintentional Sins.
- A Law of Inheritance
  - A law for the inheritance for women.
- A special Law for the Tithe
  - A Law for Offerings and Sacrifice.
- A Law for Mildew or Mold
  - The plague of Mold
- The Kingdom Laws
  - The principles for governance.

Health Laws
The Lord told Moses that life is in the blood; and therefore, it was not recommended for the people to eat the blood of anything (Leviticus 17:11).

Based on the Jewish laws of purity, a woman who has an issue of blood was prohibited to mingle with other people (Leviticus 15:19-20). It was deemed unhealthy (unclean) and the person can be judged.

However, the woman with the issue of blood defied the law by touching Jesus' garment. She knew the penalty was stoning to death, but at the time she had heard of the miracles of Jesus. Her circumstance was considered uncurable, and she had nowhere else to turn for help. Her taking the risk to touch Jesus' garment made her whole. Jesus, in His mercies and compassion, knew what she had done and turned around and blessed her because of her faith.

The Law for Sicknesses
This law was specifically for a person who had skin disease

such as leprosy. They were forbidden to stay within the camp. They were commanded to show the priest their spots and they had to be rechecked by the priests. He was the legal authority to declare them clean or unclean. The verdict was for a period of seven days. There would be a reversal concerning the spot by the priest to say that the person is clean or not contaminated (Leviticus 13:46).

A Law for Pregnancy
There is a law for the specific time of the purification for a woman after she had given birth to a child. There was a different instruction for the birth of a boy or son and the birth of a girl child; being mindful of the mother's blood issue I presume (Leviticus 12).

The bible tells us that Mary the mother of Jesus Christ did her cleansing of purification after His birth. This Jewish tradition is still practiced today and each baby is also circumcised on the eighth day.

A Special Law for the Tithe
The Lord had given this law for the welfare of the priesthood of the Levi tribe. He wanted them not to have their own lands, but to trust Him and to live off the offerings and partake of the meats at certain times. The congregation was commanded to contribute to the upkeep of the tabernacle.

A Law for Offerings and Sacrifice
A special law was given to Moses concerning the requirements of the sacrifices and offerings; the Lord desired all their offerings without spots or blemishes. Included were the priests who offered the sacrifices that were required to be without blemish.

Jesus used the widow woman as an example to emphasize her willingness to sacrifice and offer all that she possessed.

A Law for Mildew and Mold
This law was somewhat special; it implies that the Lord is concerned for other health issues, such as the danger of having mildew in the home. In the case of such a plague (as the Lord called it), the house was supposed to be shut up for seven days and afterwards, there must be another inspection by the priest (Leviticus 14:42-48). I read in a research that some scientists gave reference to a medical probability that suggested in the event of mildew or mold in the home, it has been known to cause diseases, allergies, and chronic fatigue.

> The Lord told Moses in the law that this plague was the result of the leprosy; and the owner should report this to their priests. The scripture says that, "If mildew reappears in the house after the stones have been torn out and the house scraped and re-plastered. The priest must come and inspect the house; and if the mildew has spread in the house, it must be destroyed, as it was termed as a destructive mildew."
> (Leviticus 14:42-48)

The Laws for Intentional Sins
The Lord made it clear concerning whom His judgment was against. He was especially against those people, who in their acts of wickedness, have caused the death of another person. He called them the wicked and the evil doers, as well as an idol worshipper (Numbers 5:5-7).

The Lord knows that there are many people with wrong

motives and their desire is to intentionally hurt another person. Therefore, in His judgments, there is a written Law for those people that says, "In the case of intentional sins, the wrath of God is death and separation from God." This means that there will be no light available for their path, but absolute darkness.

The Protection Laws
There are places designated for the person who had unintentionally caused the death of another person. This is known as an unintentional sin, or sins of ignorance. The Lord has granted laws for that person to seek a place of refuge from their avenger. They were commanded to live within a confined measure of boundaries; and by the law, if they were found outside their place of refuge, they would face the consequences, and their avenger could repay for his loss (Leviticus 4:1).

These protective laws are relevant for crimes committed and they are still implemented today. In the scriptures, they are identified as acts of intentional and unintentional sins. The Lord knew in this lifetime that accidents will happen and He therefore provided 'Protection Laws' in a way, ahead of time. It was also the advance notice for the judgments to the nation, according to the Judges ability to judge impartially.

The Lord instructed Moses to build cities of refuge at each border of the nation's lands in order to protect and make provision for the accused from their avengers. These refuge places were only in the case where the persons had committed un-intentional sins. It was the priest's responsibility to sanction their sentencing and they could be accepted back into society once again after the priest's death.

The Law of Inheritance
Each of the tribes of Israel were designated an allotment of land. Their inheritance was from the Lord to their fathers and the children of Israel possessed it when they entered the Promise land.

Have you ever recognized that the law of 'Inheritance' is the origin of the document called, "a Will?" It was God's idea and He had given this plan concerning the inheritance of the family to Moses. The Lord told Moses to count the men in a census before the children of Israel entered their Promise Land, and He allotted portion of land for an inheritance for each tribe and their families, according to the number of their names. The Levi tribe was the only family exempted; for the Lord had chosen them for service and a covenant of the priestly duites. They were given a city in every tribe.

In the principal of the law of inheritance, there is one significant topic found in the bible. It is about the daughters of Zelophehad. Their father had died from his own circumstances while the Israelites were wondering in the wilderness. It was noted as a peculiar incident; for Zelophehad left behind five daughters and no sons as heirs. Besides, it was mentioned that he was not among the people who murmured against God. The instruction of the Lord to Moses was to divide the land of promise between the tribes of Jacob and their generations.

Zelophehad's daughters came to Moses in the presence of all the people and appealed this directive. They requested their inheritance of the Promise Land to keep their father's lineage alive. Their opposition was questionable, and Moses knew that God had not included the women in His command. Therefore, Moses inquired of the Lord, and He did not make the decision by himself. At that moment, the Lord answered

Moses and pronounced that their case was valid in this instance. Therefore, the Lord granted them their petition and a portion of the covenant promise was given to their generations.

The Hebrew scholars have a very simple commentary on this case. They say that this was not a circumstance of greed on the girls' part. It was just a matter of their possessing the inheritance of their father. They were descendants of Manasseh, the son of Joseph, and their names were mentioned in the book of Numbers as Zelophehad daughters. Their names were Mahlah, Noa, Mic, Hoglah and Tirzah. These are very interesting names in Hebrew for a subject discussion (Numbers 27:1-11).

At the same occasion, the men began to ask Moses the question in the event of the women marrying outside their tribe. They were concerned about the transferring of the wealth to their husband's tribe. Then, Moses had to consult with the Lord on behalf of the men. In turn, the Lord instituted some restrictions on their rights to inherit the land, and He agreed that they should not be married outside their tribe.

These women's boldness has legitimate rights for the Israelite women to inherit land. Also, it has caused comfort to the misfortune of men who had no sons. Their influence in the Jewish society of the Laws of Inheritance is still alive today. However, the Lord had to place some restrictions on their rights to inherit the land. This was because of the men questioning Moses of the case in the event of these women marrying outside of their tribe. The men were concerned that the tribes' wealth would go to another tribe. And the Lord agreed that they should not be married outside their tribe. There is not much more said about these five women's boldness, except that they married within their tribe (Numbers 36:10-12).

The Kingdom Laws

In every kingdom, the king has the right to set the laws to govern the people. As an abiding citizen, you are required to obey the laws of the land or suffer the consequences of disobedience according to the laws.

God desired to be both Lord and King in the establishment of the nation of Israel. He had called Abraham and asked him to separate himself from the familiarity of his people. After Abraham obeyed, the Lord entered a covenant relationship with him and his generations. The people were given a distinction that distinguished their blessedness. Abraham's desire to be reliant upon God was seen primarily through his obedience to participate in God's kingdom laws.

The Rebellion Against the Law

What causes the judgment of God? We can look at the children of Israel as our example. Throughout history, the Jews were often disobedient to the laws of God and participated in abominable things. They often worshipped idols and did all that was dishonorable to the Lord. As a result, they entered captivity, and this led to the rulership of heathen kings who were known for their idol worshipping. Repeatedly, the children of God were warned to desist from the evil, but they rejected God.

God's covenant promise to their father Abraham was compromised, as the Israelites were not thankful to the Lord for their deliverance from the bondage of Egypt. The history of their behavioral pattern was mostly that of rebellion throughout their wilderness journeying. Moses became disgusted; he had written laws in place to create boundaries and they reject him. At some period, the Lord Himself displayed His disgust too and told Moses he would disregard them all, because of their rebellious. Yet, in humbleness, Moses pleaded with the Lord to have compassion on them, for he was mainly concerned that the Lord's reputation would be smeared by the nations.

Finally, the Lord refused to let them enter the Promised Land, even though He reminded them of their experiences and deliverance. The people blew it repeatedly, and their demise was deemed for death to the older generations.

> *The Lord said to the children of Israel, "Did not I deliver you, from the Egyptians, and from the Amorites, from the children of Ammon, and from the Philistines? The Zidonians and the Amalekites; and the Maonites, did oppress you; and you cried to me, and I delivered you out of their hands. <u>Yet you have forsaken me,</u> and served other gods: wherefore I will deliver you no more.*
> *(Judges 10:11-14)*

As mentioned before, the king of Israel was instructed to be a wise king and was commanded to write a copy of the laws that he would learn to fear the Lord. The king was to always read and carry the laws with him. He was forbidden to have many wives nor multiply wealth to himself, nor do business with their enemies. However, in the chronicles of Israel's kings, it states that most of the kings were guilty of disobeying God.

The Lord judged king Solomon, and he is a prime example of disobedience to the laws. His position was compromised during his reign. He had operated in the trading of horses with Egyptian for wealth, and he possessed many wives. Moreover, Solomon committed abominable sins as he built groves and altars, and sacrificed his children to idol gods. He was the main reason that God judged the nation and divided Israel into two states of Judah and Israel at the end of his days.

During the days of king Hezekiah, the Lord sent warnings by the prophet Isaiah. For a season he humbled himself and the Lord extended his years to fulfill the kingship covenant and blessed him with a son because he was childless. Then, after the birth of his son Manasseh, even though he had experienced the mercy of God, he became puffed up in pride and this caused his life to be terminated.

King Manasseh reigned fifty-five years, and he did worse than his father Hezekiah. His chronicle is full of his sins and abominations, and the evils that he did in the sight of the Lord. The Lord humbled Manasseh for his sins of disobeying the laws (2 Chronicles 33:9-20).

These stories of Israelites are for examples, and they portrays the judgment of God for you to reflect the similarities of the many rebellious actions of the people today. The rebellion is pertinent against the laws of a nation that governs the people. There is an apparent dishonor for parents which is seen throughout the generations. God himself gave laws to govern the nations, in order to have a respectable society (Deuteronomy 5:16).

I heard a biblical scholar say that the first law broken was *the sin of disobedience.* His explanation was that Adam and Eve had stolen the fruit of the tree in the garden. They knew it belonged to God and the simple fact was that they disobeyed the command of God. This has been a great feature in the human behavior as a whole, and somehow, obeying the "Law" is opposed by every generation.

For example, there was a story on the news recently of a woman who saw a warning sign posted saying, 'DO NOT ENTER!' and she still road her bicycle into the area. It was a swinging bridge, and at that particular time it was closed. The authorities had placed a red tape there to stop the vehicles. Nevertheless, she road pass and fell into the crack. Luckily, there were bystanders near and they were able to rescue her before she was crushed between the bridge. This is one story of how it is better to obey signs and laws. In order to avoid the possibility of disaster, the same token can be applied to the word of God.

Moses' Message

Behold, I set before you this day a blessing and a curse.
(Deuteronomy 11:26)

After the forty-years wilderness experience, Moses had a new generation. The children of Israel were about to cross over the Jordan River into their Promise land and the Lord had instructed Moses to anoint Joshua to be their new leader. Sadly, Moses was prohibited to go over Jordan because of the sin of striking the rock twice.

Moses had made known the publications of the Lord's commands and laws. The children of Israel had been given specific boundaries and were constrained to conduct themselves in a specific order. One of the laws included that when the Jewish children shall ask the meaning of keeping all these laws and feast to the Lord; the parent must tell them, "It is the commands of God and it is the sacrifice of the Lord's Passover" (Exodus 12:25-27). Moses stated that their actions of obedience will determine their consequences.

Moses knew that it was about the time of his death and he summed up his message with the credence of the blessings and the curses of the Lord. He was entreating the people to stop, and to look back or reflect, and figure out how come they did not enter their Promise land yet. He cautioned the people to exercise thoughtfulness and obedience, and he emphasized it is the pathway to righteous living. He had experienced and understood that their blessings will be to their advantage. Then, Moses concluded by telling them of the curses of God in the event of their disobedience. These scriptures are rehearsed in the bible in the book of Deuteronomy. Would you consider these conditional commands to be applicable for your life today?

> 'And it shall come to pass, if thou(you) shall hearken diligently unto the voice of the Lord thy God, to observe and to do all his commandments which I command thee(you) this Day, that the Lord thy(your) God will set thee on high above all the nations of the earth. And all the blessings shall come on thee, and overtake thee, if thou shalt hearken unto the voice of the Lord.'
> (Deuteronomy 28:3-14)

God's Blessings!
- The blessings of health.
- Blessings of children.
- Blessings of bountiful provision.
- Blessings guaranteed with showers of rain.
- Blessing over your enemies.
- Your name will be great.
- You will be the head and not the tail. You shall be above and not beneath.

God's Curses!
- Cursed shall be of the fruit of your body.
- Cursed shall be your produce of body or fruits.
- Cursed shall be your flock and provision.
- God would permit the curses of sickness, loss of life and lack.

The Lord had many conversations with Moses and on one occasion He revealed who He really was. The Lord declares that He is a *jealous* God. Therefore, His judgment is according to the extent of your actions and ungratefulness. Subsequently, Moses told all the words of the Lord to the people of Israel.

> *The Lord spoke all these words, saying, 'I Am the Lord thy God, which brought you out of the land of Egypt, and out of the house of bondage. I Am a jealous God.'*
> *(Exodus 20:3-17)*

One of the saddest things about the human nature is that their disobedience creates our actual experience of suffering. I have noticed that we make it habitual to blame the devil for everything. However, I am becoming aware that it is not always the devil's fault. I am just acknowledging the fact that he keeps complaining to the Lord about things outside his control. Something to consider: maybe he is sometimes in the right.

In your refusal to obey the Lord, it makes God's rulership over your life limited and it will bring you into disagreement with the Lord, which can result in His judgment (Deuteronomy 28:15-67).

Chapter 4
THE GOD OF JUSTICE

Justice and judgement are the habitation of thy throne: mercy and truth shall go before thy face.
(Psalm 89:14)

The Lord Jesus is a God of Justice. The bible says that He is our Defense and our Mediator and He functions as our Lawyer to plead our cases before the Father.

The word *mediator* means *"a go-between, an arbiter, a reconciler, or an intermediator."* It also means *"the one who intervenes between two persons, either in order to make or restore peace and friendship; or for the ratifying of a covenant."* Jesus stands as our advocate for the demands of the Father God. Moreover, He is our defense means that He defends us from the accuser, and He resists attacks on our behalf. Besides, Jesus stands as a man understanding our human limitations and frailty (Hebrews 4:15-16).

There is one God, and one mediator between God and men, the man Christ Jesus.
(2 Timothy 2:5)

The Lord desires that the believers would not overlook His character of Him being a God of justice and judgment. In the heavenly courtroom, God the Father sits upon a throne, and Jesus our Lord pleads our cases as a Lawyer. According to the biblical history perspective, the Lord Jesus has won every case against the accuser of the brethren. This is a reminder that during Passover, on the hill of Calvary's cross, Jesus shed His blood. Then, when you humbly repent, Jesus forgives and He places His precious blood as the evidence for your restoration; and your name is cleared from the laws of sin and death. In His act of obedience, Jesus saves you from every sin and temptation, and from every attack of your enemies. Hence, His everlasting covenant of salvation will cover you eternally.

It struck me, like a ton of bricks, as I was writing this chapter, "Do you realize that the Devil has no answer for the blood of Jesus Christ!" He freezes at the name of Jesus; and demons tremble at His name. This is one of the revelations that is the most important thing to remember.

In a few verses the Lord explained His justice towards the affliction of the widow or the fatherless child. He acknowledged that if He ever hear their cry in any wise coming up to Him, then His wrath shall wax hot, and He will kill the oppressor with His sword (Exodus 22:22-24). This means that God is passionate for the widows and orphans.

In the book of Hebrews, the apostle Paul declares that God is Judge of all, and through Him, the spirits of the just men are made perfect. He explained the distinction of the sprinkling of the animal's blood that Moses performed on the altar; it was the foreshadow of Jesus Christ, who is the mediator of the new covenant, and He is the blood of sprinkling of the New Testament (Hebrews 12:24).

Jesus the Lawyer

For Christ is not entered into the holy places made with hands, which are the figures of the true; but into

> *heaven itself, now to appear in the presence of God*
> *for us.*
> *(Hebrews 9:24)*

On this day, before Jesus' ascension, He had made the arrangement with God the Father for us to have an Advocate and Comforter to be with us forever. The Holy Ghost is the divine person of the trinity He requested (John 14:16). Jesus Christ your intercessor, and the Holy Spirit will enforce your destiny and the blessings that God has planned for your life.

> *But this man (Jesus Christ), because he continued ever, had an unchangeable priesthood. Wherefore he is able also to save those to the uttermost that come unto God by him, seeing he ever live to make intercessions for them.*
> *(Hebrews 7:24-25)*

> *It is Christ that died, yea rather, that is risen again, who is even at the right of God, who also make intercession for us.*
> *(Romans 8:34)*

These stories that are included will be a source of encouragement for you, in times that you experience trouble in your life, you will trust and pray to the Lord of Justice. It is evident that the Lord fought many of David's battles, as he desperately needed a lawyer, especially when Saul persistently pursued David's life in an act of jealousy and fear. This was derived from David's victory over the Philistines. David refused to be the one to take Saul's life, even though David had an ample opportunity to retaliate. He was humble and gave Saul honor because he understood the anointing of the king over Israel, and hence, David allowed the Lord to fight his battles. The bible says that the Lord allowed the death of Saul in due season. You would think that David should have rejoiced over Saul's death, but he was humble, and grieved at the news of Saul and Jonathan's death.

> *The Lord is my defense; and my God is the rock of my refuge. And He shall bring upon them their own iniquity, and shall cut them off in their wickedness.*
> *(Psalms 94:22)*

On many occasions Isaac, the son of Abraham, needed a lawyer. There was famine in the land and Isaac wanted to go down to Egypt. The Lord appeared to Isaac and told him to remain in the land of Philistine, so he would not make the same mistake his father did. The Lord had intended for Isaac to inherit the Land of Promise of his father Abraham. In obedience, and in the famine, Isaac grew and became very prosperous. Subsequently, he experienced many calamities with the Philistines. The people envied Isaac and they retaliated by filling up the wells that the servants of his father Abraham dug. Their intentions were to drive Isaac away from each area he tried to settle in. Nevertheless, in His justice, the Lord blessed them as the servants kept on digging wells, and water sprang up everywhere they went (Genesis 26).

This seemed like a typical legal setting in the case of the woman caught in the act of adultery; and she needed a Lawyer. On this day, the leaders had brought her to Jesus and they had asked His opinion concerning the matter. At this setting, she was the accused; evidence was stacked up against her, while her accusers stood awaiting her judgment. They wanted Jesus to respond to her situation as a temptation for His demise. The issue was that Jesus saw the circumstance from a logical point of view, and He recognized that there was an error; for this case involved the actions of two persons. However, there was only one partner present and the other partner was not in attendance. Perhaps, the reason for the male partner's absence was that he had been one of their leaders or he was someone's marital partner (John 8:1-11).

As Jesus proceeded in her defense, He stooped down and began to write in the dust; for He knew the intent of their hearts. Have you ever wondered what He wrote in the dust? The Hebrew sages say that it was possible that Jesus was writing the verse of Jeremiah 17:13 in the dust. They say that Jesus began writing their names and their sins that they had committed. The accusers at this incident were well-known teachers, and Scribes and Pharisees who studied the scriptures. They were familiar with the scripture Jesus wrote in the dust; and they we guilty of rejecting the ministry of Jesus.

> *O Lord, the hope of Israel, all that forsake thee shall be ashamed, and they that depart from me shall be written in the earth, because they have forsaken the Lord, the fountain of living waters.*
> *(Jeremiah 17:13)*

After writing, Jesus stood up, and He asked, "If anyone was without sin, that they should cast the first stone." The bible says that they all trickled away, one by one quietly, because they were humiliated and guilty of their own sins. Jesus, in

His mercy, did not condemn her, but cautioned her to sin no more. Maybe, Jesus had in some way understood her plight; for it was mentioned in the gospels that she was possessed with seven devils, where Jesus, on another occasion, had casted the evil spirits out of her.

> *As Jesus said, 'You judge after the flesh; I judge no man. And yet, if I judge, my judgement is true: for I am not alone, but I and my Father that sent me.'*
> *(John 8:14-18)*

It was in the next few scriptures following this incident that Jesus spoke to His disciples and told them of His position as it pertained to His judgments and justice. This was an enlightening lesson to the believer who finds themselves in a dilemma; it is a way of caution to the judgmental attitude of another person. On many occasions it is the natural mindset to be able to see the outward appearance – only God knows the heart of a man. Therefore, it is worthwhile to allow the Holy Spirit to guide you in the way of the Spirit of discernment, and you can leave the task of judgment to the Lord.

Joshua's Need for a Lawyer

The story is told of Zachariah the prophet, who had seen in a vision the detail account of the judicial court system in heaven. Zachariah detailed a case with Joshua the High Priest and Satan the accuser. It seemed like the devil's accusation was standing against Joshua's position as the leader for the Israelites. The scripture describes the scene as a battle for the priestly position and the allegations of the accuser that comes against the servants of the Lord.

The God of Justice

He showed me Joshua the high priest standing before the angel of the Lord, and Satan standing at his right hand to resist him. And the Lord said unto Satan, "The Lord rebuke you, Satan! The Lord that had chosen Jerusalem rebuke you! Is it not a brand plucked from the fire?"

Now Joshua was clothed with filthy garments and was standing before the angel.

> *Then, He answered and spoke to those who stood before Him, saying, "Take away the filthy garments from him." And to him He said, "See. I have removed your iniquity from you, and I will clothe you with a change of garment."*
>
> *And I said, "Let them put a clean turban on his head." So, they put a clean turban on his head, and they put the clothes on him. And the Angel of the Lord stood by him.*
>
> *Then the Angel of the Lord admonished Joshua, saying, Thus says the Lord of Hosts:*
>
> *"If you will walk in My ways, And If you will keep My command, then you shall also judge My house. And you shall have charge of My courts; I will give you places to walk among these that stand by.*
> *(Zachariah 3:1-7)*

History reveals that there were many high priests before the birth of the Messiah. This high priest, Joshua, was from an era after Eleazar the high priest. The priests were responsible for the spiritual and physical aspect of the Temple of God. The Temple was first destroyed around 490 BC and Joshua was chosen by God to be a part of the restoration of the second Temple. Officially, he was anointed to be the high priest and Satan approached God to accused him of being unclean spiritually. Satan's objective was to hinder Joshua from doing God's work. The Lord had chosen Joshua to re-establish the city of Jerusalem and the tactic of Satan was to stop the rebuilding from happening.

The devil was standing before God to abort the work by accusing Joshua of being unrighteous. This accusation is the statement that will edify you; for it is essential for you to be clean and holy in order to do the Will of God. The devil is positioned to try and stop you, and without the condition of sanctification he wants to delay what the Lord desires to do through you.

The Lord responded to Satan with a rebuke, in Joshua's case. It was a rebuke not for Joshua's sake, but for the sake of Jerusalem to be rebuilt. Joshua needed to be cleaned up in order that the devil would have no legal resistance against him again. Joshua was unclean in some ways, because he doubted God's promises; and there was fear in his heart, because the children of Israel had constantly rebelled. This led them into exile and the temple was destroyed in the first instant. Therefore, it was imperative that Joshua had to sanctify himself, and the people, as the accuser had a legal right to resist him.

The final scene was the cleansing process of Joshua by the angel of God, as they strengthened him for the purpose of his destiny. The prophet Zachariah also saw himself in the vision, as he began to cleanse Joshua as well. Zachariah proclaimed that they should place a clean turban on Joshua's head. The scholars say that this means that the spiritual atmosphere was cleansed as the angels put clean garments on Joshua and the covering upon his head. This was a representation of the freedom Joshua received from anything that the devil could have accused him.

The performance on the behalf of Joshua to make him clean was therefore to enable him to stay clean and walk in righteousness before the Lord. He was then granted authority and was charged to judge in the courts of the house of the Lord to set things in order upon the earth. I heard someone say that we need the angelic and prophetic sanction as we are to be cleansed for God's work. The Lord as our Justice can enforce His blessing in your life and in your family. He can also enforce His blessings in your church and your community.

The Accuser

After reading the many accusations of the devil against the saints of God, I was inspired to scrutinize his strategy. In the book of Ezekiel 28:14, the scripture says that Satan operated in the courts of heaven. He is known as Lucifer, and he walked on the fiery stones. Before his fall, he was granted charge to gather evidence and present it before God's throne. Then, God would render a verdict based upon the evidence presented (Job 1:7).

> *How are you fallen from heaven, O Lucifer, son of the morning! How are you cut down to the ground, which did weaken the nations! For you have said in*

> *thine heart, "I will ascend into heaven, I will exalt my throne above the stars of God: I will sit down on the mount of the congregation, in the sides of the north: I will ascend above the heights of the clouds; I will be like the most High. Yet you shall be brought down to hell, to the sides of the pit.*
> *(Isaiah 14:12-15)*

> *You are the anointed cherub who covers; and I have set you there: You were upon the holy mountain of God; you have walked up and down in the midst of the stones of fire.*
> *(Ezekiel 28:14)*

The scriptures confirm that the devil has a job; he still walks to-and-fro throughout the earth. However, Satan can only devour when he has a legal right. This explains why good people have had bad things happen to them. The Devil must possess legal right in order to accuse you before the Father, and according to his perspective of your generational history, he seeks the right to accuse you. Therefore, only the blood of Jesus can sanction his rights (1 Peter 5:8).

My Desire for the Lawyer

To illustrate an urgent need for Jesus my lawyer, let me share the events of my own personal life. I was the youngest child in my family. The stigma of sibling rivalry was rampant in the home. I was numbered among the children that usually seemed to have no voice. There were times when I could only talk to Jesus about my dilemma.

On Sundays, we attended church as children, but my family did not recognize that I was taking the concept of church and the bible seriously. The relationship aspect of Jesus Christ as your personal Savior was not emphasized in my home. I had a lot of questions in my head and I often asked my Godmother for answers (and she somewhat helped to put some things into perspective for me). I began to recognize that my life was a type of religious culture. No one was committed to the significance of salvation, therefore, the knowledge of it was limited to whatever our priest had spoken.

Then during my elementary school years, there was a bible class held once a week where I learned about the Lord and His salvation plan from one of the lessons. I accepted Jesus Christ as my Lord and Savior at the age of twelve; I felt that there was something special about Jesus, and I wanted Him to give me an opportunity to do something for Him. At first, I wanted to be close to Him, and I would venture off to my friend's house, and we would go to the local church in the town nearby. A few weeks into my little scheme, my mom found out and I was warned of consequences if I returned there. My mom was not equipped for my change in belief, and she voiced her negative sentiments. She felt the religious group was going to indoctrinate me at my age and said that it was more feasible to attend the family church. Everyone knew my relatives (and it was for generations), but she did not attend herself. Their culture was very firm in my home, therefore, to avoid a whooping I complied to her wishes.

At the beginning, without any consideration of the consequences, I had plunged into the faith of Jesus Christ. I was just a teen and the outcome of my decision cost me greatly. As I recall, the family disapproval and rejection were mostly intense. Then, I had begun to exempt myself from the normal activities with my family and friends. It became difficult to have any spiritual support and I began to get distracted as I approached my adult years.

The resistance of a lack of spiritual morals began to stir me into the opposite direction. I can relate to teenagers who experience this kind of rejection because of their faith in Jesus Christ. One day, I had heard pastor Benny talk of his experience with his family after accepting Jesus Christ as his personal Savior. His story gave me the courage to trust the Lord to transform my life and I began to pray and seek the Lord to restore my faith again. In time, as I continued to read the bible and pray, Jesus came and restored me in His mercy and grace. He has forgiven me of all my transgressions and sins.

Jesus Christ is my lawyer and He fought every legal battle and reclaimed the rights to my life. He has set me free and His blood pardoned all my sins and the accusation that Satan had against me was cancelled. Today, I can testify that "God is Faithful" and I believe that the "Greater One" lives inside of me. I believe that Jesus Christ died on Calvary's cross and He shed His blood, and He stands as a mediator to speak on our behalf to enforce our destiny. My faith and trust are in Jesus Christ.

*There is therefore now no condemnation to them
which are in Christ Jesus, who walk not after
the flesh, but after the Spirit.
(Romans 8:1)*

For He made Him who knew no sin to be sin for us, that we might become the righteousness of God in Him. (2 Corinthians 5:21)

My little children, these things I write to you, so that you may not sin, And if anyone sins, we have an Advocate (Mediator) with the Father, Jesus Christ the righteous.
(1 John 2:1)

Peter Needed the Lawyer

In the bible there is a story written of an apostle named, Simon Peter. He loved Jesus Christ and was destined to do an incredible work for the Lord. Peter's ability to fulfill the plans of God was obvious and Satan, the accuser, tried to withstand him. He went out on a rampage to disqualify Peter from the mission. Jesus knew of Satan's scheme and warned Peter of the opposition against the Lord's agenda. Jesus told Peter that He saw Satan desiring to sift him as wheat, but He had prayed for him, that his faith would not fail him (Luke 22:31-32).

    This conversation took place before Jesus was crucified, and although Peter was forewarned, he denied that he knew Him. Peter must have felt awful and he repented. Then, Jesus in His compassion gave Peter the keys to the kingdom of heaven.

    Peter's ministry was spread across the whole earth, and the evidence was that multitudes were saved, and great deliverances took place as the kingdom of God was strengthened by the power of the blood of Jesus Christ. Thus, the testimony of salvation lives on today. The apostle Peter attested that the eyes of the Lord are over the righteous, and His ears are opened to their prayers. He added that the face of the Lord is against them that do evil (1 Peter 3:12). For Jesus is the same yesterday, today and forever, Amen.

Chapter 5
THE WILL OF GOD

God is not a man, that he should lie; neither the son of man that he should repent: had he said, and shall he not do it? Or had he spoken, and shall not make it good?
(Numbers 23:19)

There is a character design within a man that is known as your willpower, and it initiates your decisions in life. Well, the same can be said of the Lord God of the Universe; for He functions in His willpower and in His authority.

The Lord is never disillusioned by your willpower and weaknesses. The way that the *Will of God* operates in our life captivates my comprehension. He is known as the All-sufficient One and this concept will change your perspective. In each circumstance regarding life in general it will make me ponder at the many cases that the Lord was trying to get my attention. This topic will enlighten you of the many times that you have tried your own willpower and realized that it had not gotten anything under your control without the Lord's help.

There are primarily two functions of God's Will in operation in our life which are notable to discuss: "*His Perfect Will and His Permissive Will.*"

(1) His Perfect Will
God's perfect Will is His Divine plan for your life. His plans are written in His book in heaven concerning your birth and

the fulfillment of your destiny. God's desire is to divinely connect you to the people with whom you should encounter on the pathway of your life, as your gifts are linked to His Perfect Will. The Lord has a great interest in your destiny, especially concerning your partner in marriage. The scriptures admonish you to trust in the Lord with all your heart and in all your ways, and He will direct your path.

    A perfect example was the story of the marriage of Isaac and his wife Rebecca. For God's covenant with Abraham to be accomplished, His will and His plan had guided Abraham to choose of a bride of his kindred for his son, Isaac. In this situation, Isaac's godly parents desired to please the Lord and he trusted their wisdom (Genesis 24).

> *Before I formed thee in the belly, I knew thee; and before thou came out of the womb I sanctified thee, and I ordained thee a prophet unto the nations.*
> *(Jeremiah 1:5)*

> *For thou has possessed my reins: thou has covered me in my mother's womb. I will praise thee, for I am fearfully and wonderfully made, marvelous are thy works; and that my soul know right well.*
> *(Psalm 139:13-14)*

Before the foundation of the world, God's *perfect will* was predestined for His only son, Jesus Christ, to be born and die on a cross. The Lord instructed Moses and told him how to conduct the preparation for their feasts in the book of Leviticus. The Lamb was to be sacrificed outside of the camp as a foreshadow of what the crucifixion of the Lamb of God would be like. Jesus Christ became an outcast through the rejection and the unbelief of the children of Israel.

The Hebrew scriptures show in the book of Isaiah 53 that Jesus was that sacrificial Lamb. He was called, the Branch, who would rule as Judge of the people. The servant that the prophet Isaiah had mentioned in the scriptures was the Messiah. He prophesied that "He is despised and rejected of men; a man of sorrows and acquainted with grief" (Isaiah 53:2-11).

> *He was afflicted, yet he opened not his mouth: He is brought as a lamb to the slaughter, and as a sheep before her shearers is dumb, so He opened not his mouth.*
> *(Isaiah 53:7)*

(2) His Permissive Will

The Lord is a gentleman and so is His Holy Spirit. Therefore, He would not force His Will upon you. Instead, He will function in His *permissive will*, when you have no desire for His perfect Will. As a merciful God, He will allow things to be manifested to meet your desires, however, *this does not mean that it is His will.* Furthermore, the Lord will simply sanction those occurrences with His approval that materializes and can be unpleasant to you.

It will be worthwhile to inquire of the Lord; for His counsel and His 'Perfect Will' in your lifetime desires. In His love and compassion, He does not require much. He might give you an advice here and there, if He desires. However, the fundamental things in your life, such as the clothes you wear and the colors you desire are your choice. In addition, you are permitted to choose the pet you like and the car you want to drive. Nevertheless, the Lord is concerned for your destiny, your life partner, and for your soul. It is your responsibility to check with Him for guidance of the things pertaining to your life.

God is our Creator; though this is often ignored until circumstances arises in your life, especially when there are no reasonable explanations for it. For instance, the loss of a love one, or loss of a job; somehow, it is easy for you to blame the devil for everything, or perhaps you have blamed God.

One of the common phrases found in the scriptures is, *"They did not inquire of the Lord."* The bible says that God did not approve of many things that the people had done over the years, even in the time of Jesus. In some of the stories you have read, the Lord had permitted many sad incidences because of their evil desires.

The Distinction of the Wills

When the Lord revealed Himself as Adonai to Moses, He distinctly resounded *'His Will'* in the levels of His deliverance of the children of Israel. Then, the Lord said: *I will bring you out from under the burden. I will rescue you out of bondage. I will redeem you with a stretched out arm and with great judgments: I will take you to Me for a people, and I will be to you a God* (Exodus 6:6-7). This implies that the Lord has a Will to be a covenant keeper.

In many biblical accounts, the Lord had judged the people for their defiance towards Him. God's *permissive will* was described as the people refused to obey His instructions.

The vital role of events that transpired were of instant judgment, or in a time set by the Lord. Today, as you function in your selfish ambitions, it shows that the Lord allows His 'permissive will' to operate in your life.

God's *permissive will* was in the instance where the people of Israel desired a king. The story says that the elders of Israel gathered against the prophet Samuel and they had demanded him to anoint them a king. The circumstances leading up to their demand was that they knew that Samuel had judged over them many years and he was becoming older. In the Lord's divine plan, He wants to be their King and had never wanted them to be governed by an earthly king. They continued to rebel against the Lord, so He spoke through the prophet Samuel to explain the consequences of having a king like the other nations. Nonetheless, they rebelled and subsequently, the Lord appointed Saul as king to rule over them.

> *And the Lord said unto Samuel, listen to the voice of the people in all they say to you, for they have not rejected you, but they have rejected me, that I should not reign over them.*
> *(1 Samuel 8: 4-10)*

The story with Job in the bible seems overwhelming and the activity of Satan the accuser against Job was difficult to comprehend. Why would the Lord permit Job's catastrophe? The story shows that God had sanctioned His *permissive will* in the case of the accuser. The scriptures say that the Lord asked Satan where he had been. And his response was, "From going to and fro in the earth." Then, the Lord inquired of the devil about His servant Job; it sounded like there was confidence in the question, as He knew that Job's integrity was faithfulness.

The Lord knows that Satan walks back and forth searching out for those people who have a kingdom destiny. As I mentioned before, Satan can only devour when he has a legal reason. These incidences somehow were a great challenge for Job and there were so many unpleasant occurrences during these tests. I wondered if Job was spiritually unprepared after so many trials; for the bible says that he felt unworthy of the blessings and protection that he did receive from the Lord (Job 13:15).

Nevertheless, Job mustered up and maintained strength and endured to the end. The bible also declared that brother Job later became victorious and his reward was great. It was an encouragement to read that Job lived for many years after this and was blessed with sons and daughters. The sages say that Job's three daughters were known to be the most beautiful women of their time. The blessings Job received was a double portion for his troubles and he lived to fellowship with his fourth generation of sons' sons.

> *The Lord is not slack concerning His promise, as some men count slackness; but is longsuffering to us-ward, not willing that any should perish, but all should come to repentance.*
> *(1 Peter 3:9)*

Joseph was the son of Jacob, and during his adolescent years, he was betrayed by his brothers and was sold into slavery. It is a touching story. I often wonder, "Why would the Lord allow His *permissive will* to let him experience such horrific things?" The answer is rather baffling to me and I still try to understand the ways of God. Seemingly, it was God's divine purposes, and He was working out His plan before the time of famine in the land.

The terrific account of Joseph's life was a divine plan, and there was an inclusion for him to be placed into prison and to be forgotten for many years. Then, the Lord also planned a scenario of a couple of dreams further into his stay in the prison. The Pharaoh of Egypt had two dreams which he needed to remember and to be interpreted. This caused a prompting in the butler's heart to remember and mention his experience in the prison to the Pharaoh. This made the Pharaoh send for Joseph to come out of the prison to give the interpretation of his dreams.

The Hebrew scholars says that God's divine plan for Joseph was to be a foreshadow and a type of a Savior. They suggest that Joseph's role was to be a deliverer for his family and people during the days of famine. Besides, the circumstance of his difficult years were a testimony of the goodness and faithfulness of God (Genesis 40-47).

> *And Joseph said to them, Fear not: for am I in the place of God? But for you, you thought evil against me; but God meant it unto good, to bring to pass as it is this day, to save much people alive.*
> *(Genesis 50:19-20)*

There was a promise made to Abraham as he made a covenant with God. The Lord promised Abraham that He would make his generations into a great nation. Abraham chose to obey and trust the Lord in all his ways, even though he was childless. In his old age, Abraham had received his miracle child and he named him Isaac. Abraham taught his son Isaac the things of God and he grew into a young man. Then Abraham was concerned for his son to have a marital partner, according to the Will of the Lord his God (Genesis 24:2-4).

Isaac became a father and he had two children. He wanted his sons, Jacob and Esau, to choose wives of their genealogy. The boys knew the stories of God and the covenant promise to their grandfather Abraham. They both lived during the days of Abraham; for he died when they were about thirty years old. The scriptures say that only Jacob obeyed his father and mother, and took a wife of their lineage (Genesis 26:34-35).

His brother Esau's rebellion caused his parents grief. The bible says that the Lord declared, "Jacob I love and Esau I hated." This sounded like harsh words, but the word was used in the text as a result of Esau's actions to choose his own will. In the Hebrew writings it suggests that the Lord was saying that He 'despises or disapproves' of Esau's behavior. It was the *permissive will* of the Lord that caused Esau to live in his state of rebellion, because in those days they were stoned for disobedience to the commands of the Lord.

King Saul walked in the *'permissive will'* of God. He was the chosen king over Israel, but his character was flawed with several issues of disobedience; these were recorded and they caused him to be rejected as king. In one incident, Saul had failed by disobeying the Lord's command to destroy all the Amalekites for the evil Amalek had done to the children of God while they were in the wilderness journey. He chose instead to keep the best spoils of the Amalekites for himself and to sacrifice them to God in his disobedience. All the Lord wanted from Saul was his obedience, and therefore God rejected his sacrifices.

The Will of God

'Obedience is better than sacrifice.'
(1 Samuel 15:22)

In an earlier chapter, the story was told of King Manasseh who was the son of King Hezekiah (2 Kings 21). He began to reign at twelve years old and grew up in a prophet's home. He knew all the prophets of his father's reign. Yet, the bible says that he did that which was evil in the sight of the Lord. He was a disobedient king, and he chose his own will and used enchantments, familiar spirits and wizards; like king Saul. Instead of seeking the will of God, he set graven images of groves in the house of the Lord, of which the Lord told David and his son, Solomon, not to do. The Lord knew when to convert his permissive will to his perfect will in Manasseh's life.

> *In this house, and in Jerusalem, which I have chosen before all the tribes of Israel, will I put my name forever - saith the Lord.*
> *(2 Chronicles 33:7)*

In the previous stories, most of the people were operating in disobedience and rebellion towards the Lord. Those people were disapproved and despised by God and were separated as a resulted. The Prophet Hosea, like Moses, reminded the people not to forget the mercies and compassion of the Lord (Hosea 13:6).

However, there are people who chose to walk in the 'Will of God.' The scriptures say that amongst them were the prophets and some kings, who inquired of the Lord, and they took the Lord's council regarding each battle and the welfare of the people. The Prophet Jeremiah is numbered amongst the obedient prophets, and testimony of his life came before he was even born. God knew what type of man he would become (Jeremiah 1:5). Jeremiah is a prophet for our times. During the times of the captivity of Israel, He was a voice for the Lord to many kings.

Jesus the son of God is our ultimate example among the many obedient ones. For Jesus humbled Himself as a man to die as a sacrifice in our place. There was Abraham a friend of God, who by faith when he was called by God, went to a place not known, and there he received for an inheritance (Hebrews 11:8). Then there was Moses the deliverer, whom by faith, trusted God's leading to deliver the children of Israel out of Egypt. And Joshua, who believes the Lord by faith, and walked around the wall of Jericho seven times, and afterward, saw the wall fall for him to conquer the land.

I could go on and on, for instance with King David, and Samuel the prophet. Also, Rebecca the mother of Jacob and Esau, who carried two nations in her belly, as she is trusting the Lord would reveal which twin would rule over the other. Moreover, Jacob's name was changed to Israel as he mustered courage to wrestle the angel for his breakthrough and blessings.

I pray that you will acknowledge your position and recognize that you have the will to choose and to acknowledge that the Lord has the right to His own Will. However, it is better to inquire of the will of the Lord for your life and godliness in Christ Jesus.

My people are destroyed for lack of knowledge: because thou rejected knowledge, I will reject thee, that thou be no priest to me: seeing thou has forgotten the law of the thy God, I will also forget thy children.
(Hosea 4:6)

Chapter 6
OUR DELIVERER AND KING

The Lord knows how to deliver the godly out of temptations, and to reserve the unjust unto the day of judgment to be punished.
(2 Peter 2:9)

Jesus declares that He is the First and the Last, the beginning and the End of all creation! In Hebrew culture Jesus or 'Yeshua' is the only 'One' that has this testimony as the son of God, therefore, He has the authority to pronounce justice and judgment.

The truth is that everyone is valuable in God's eyes and He despises all injustice passionately.

However, His justice and judgment are restricted, as it is dependent on how you receive His light. The scriptures say that the Lord will bless those who walk in His commands and in the light of His countenance. His desire is that none should perish, but all would come to repentance.

Repentance means a*n action to return to the original One who created you.* True repentance is related to holiness. The power of repentance is to cause a change to your future. You cannot continue to repeat the sins you practice; for such is not true repentance.

As our Messiah-King, He does possess a kingdom, and His request is to have a certain type of citizens to be a part of His kingdom. In the word of God, He has revealed the set boundary within His kingdom. Outside those boundaries, it is His mercies that cause us not to be consumed; for the Lord is compassionate, faithful and committed to fight for your soul.

> *It is of the Lord's mercies that we are not consumed, because his compassions fail not. They are new every morning: great is thy faithfulness.*
> *(Lamentations 3:22-23)*

Some people say that the Old Testament has been done away with. Notwithstanding, there is a peculiar book that Moses wrote that is connected to the laws of successful living. In the book of Leviticus, the Lord had many valuable reasons that He had placed the natural boundaries. For instance, all nations of the world have borders, and this gives them a state to claim, and the right to govern that territory. Should anyone cross their boundaries, the ensuing nation would require that they must comply to the laws of that new territory. It is accurate to say that there are many fundamental laws found in the scriptures that are applicable to today.

In one of the stories of Moses, when he had encountered the Lord, the bible declared that the Lord revealed Himself to him as the God of "Justice and Truth." This experience happened at mount Sinai. In this scenario, Moses had a desire to know God and he wanted to encounter the One that was calling him to deliver His people. Moses was called to lead the Hebrew people out of Egypt into the wilderness and into an unknown place that God called their Promise Land. And as their deliverer, he needed tangible evidence to relate to; for the people were "a piece of work."

The Lord, the Lord God, merciful and gracious, longsuffering, and abundant in goodness and truth, Keeping mercy for thousands, forgiving iniquity and transgressions and sin, and that will by no means clear the guilty; visiting the iniquity of the fathers upon the children's children, unto the third and fourth generation.
(Exodus 34:5-8)

Moses' Need for the Deliverer

The case of Korah's rebellion and conspiracy against the Lord and Moses is a prime situation for the justice of the Lord. Moses was the cousin of Korah and he had rebelled against the authority of Moses; for he thought Moses was exalting himself above the people. Korah had abrasively questioned the office of the priesthood, as he felt that he should have been given the position instead of Aaron. His rebellion was towards the Lord, who instructed Moses to anoint Aaron as High Priest.

The rebellion intensified as the brothers from the tribe of Rueben (Dothan, Abiram and On), and the sons of Levi, had gathered with a force of two hundred and fifty men of prominence from among the tribes. The confrontation of Korah's murmuring had instigated chaos and mutiny within the camp. This caused a swift and dreadful judgment to occur within the camp; the Lord threatened to destroy all the people. Nevertheless, Moses and Aaron pleaded with the Lord for the people to be spared.

The Lord told Moses to separate the people away from those that were rebelling. After the people ran away from the scene, the supernatural happened as the earth opened its mouth and swallowed up Korah and his family; and another miracle happened as the earth closed its mouth. Only the Lord could have done such an earthquake. It is not normal for the earth to close after an earthquake. Moses could not have opened the earth; it was a miracle (Numbers 16).

The Lord was furious, as He sent a fire afterwards, and consumed the two hundred and fifty men that were around the tents. Nevertheless, on the following day, after the people had seen the judgment of the Lord, they still continued to murmur and accuse Moses of killing the men. Consequently, the Lord sent a plague and the scripture says that a great number of people lost their lives. The justice of the Lord seemed vigorous for the sins of men. At that time, Moses and Aaron prayed and gave offerings to the Lord which caused the plague to cease.

The account of the children of Israel's rebellion against the Lord and the judgments of God are summarized in Psalm 106. The scriptures say that the Lord sent leanness to their souls and gave them what they wanted. Thus, they became spiritually weak as their souls diminished. This is a lesson you need to be aware of today. It was a great judgment because the people murmured and believe not, nor hearkened to the voice of the Lord.

The Laws Against Injustice

The Lord is a Just God. We have touched on this subject a little earlier, but the emphasis of this Law includes the protection of injustice between the rich and the poor. He is supreme because His desire was to ensure that justice will prevail amongst the people in order to prevent the advantage or disadvantage of one person against another in their wealth and lifestyle.

The scholar says that there were many cases of injustice operating in the land in the time of Jesus. He had experienced it Himself and knew the unfairness that the children of Israel experienced in Egypt. The Lord knows that this injustice will still transpire today, and therefore, a system of law is put in place.

A very substantial one is the laws for justice; this law includes that a person who worked as a hired servant will receive wages on time. There is another law against a man who would not allow the ox that was working to eat grain of the field (Deuteronomy 24:14-15).

In the case of the Israelite people, the Lord had pronounced justice and judgment against the Amalekites for their sins. During the days of the deliverance of the Hebrew children, as they went forth towards their journey to the promised land, the children of Amalek had heartlessly attacked them. Therefore, the Lord told Moses that the children of Israel were to destroy Amalek's generation; He declared that His judgment against them will be a memorial forever (Exodus 17:8-16).

And Joshua discomfited Amalek and his people with the edge of the sword. And the Lord said unto Moses, Write this for a memorial in a book, and rehearse it in the ears of Joshua: For I will utterly put out the remembrance of Amalek from under the heavens.
(Exodus 17:13-14)

The Lord's judgment for injustice was also pronounced on the Ammonites and Moabites; they were not allowed to come into the congregation of God. They had hired Balaam to curse the children of Israel because of their fear of them when they heard of the victories of Israel conquering the land. Justice for Israel had to prevail for ten generations as the Lord commanded Moses. However, through the mercy of God, He had turned their curse into a blessing to His people (Deuteronomy 23:2-3). Many generations later, the Lord had overruled His judgment, as His compassion was shown to Ruth the Moabite at her conversion to Judaism. She became the great grandmother of king David (Ruth 4:17-22).

> *He shall stand at the right hand of the poor, to save him from those that condemn his soul.*
> *(Psalms 109:31)*

The Judicial System of God

The scholars say that today the judicial system that operates in the world was derived from the judicial courtroom pattern in heaven. According to the prophets, the laws of God still stand. The court setting still consisted of the Judge, the attorney, the witnesses, the jury, the bailiff, the recorder and the accused.

Jesus had a lot to say about the unjust practices of mankind in the New Testament when He mentioned that God is a Judge. However, some people will argue that the laws of God are obsolete today. His justice shall prevail over all sin and wickedness. For God sees every injustice you will ever experience, and He will perform His justice on your behalf in due season.

Our Deliverer and King

Jesus practiced many of the laws of Moses that were in place for His righteous living. According the principles of the bible, Jesus came in the beginning of His ministry to John the Baptist and was baptized in the Jordan River under John's ministry. John 16:16 says, "He that believes and is baptized shall be saved." Jesus also gave the command to His followers that they should teach and baptize in the name of the Father, and of the Son and of the Holy Ghost (Matthew 28:18-20).

Jesus was then led to the wilderness for forty days and forty nights. Similarly, Moses went forty days up to mount Sinai in the wilderness to commune with God. There in the wilderness Satan approached Him and used the tactics of the promises of God to tempt Jesus. Jesus quoted God's laws from the Old Testament to defend His faith. The sages say that each believer must experience their wilderness in order to apply the laws of righteous living.

Jesus exercised the justice of God throughout His walk upon the earth. He prayed and sought the council of His Father daily. He made clear His position concerning the laws of God. In some occasions, He exhibited that love was more important than the laws. For instance, He did the healing of the sick on the Sabbath. In our walk with the Lord, the pathway that Jesus walked will be like the experiences of justice and injustice.

'Thou shall not live by bread alone, but by every word that proceeded from the mouth of God do man live.'
(Deuteronomy 8:3)

The mouth of the righteous speaks wisdom, and his tongue talks of judgement. The law of his God is in his heart; none of his steps shall slide.
(Psalms 37:30-13)

In His humanity, Jesus operated as a citizen of Israel and obeyed the laws of the land. He paid the tribute to Caesar and He avoided offending the tax-collectors. In one instance, He told Peter to go and get the money out of the fish's mouth (Matthew 17:27). The revelation of God's justice was foreshadowed in the miracle of the coin.

For the Tabernacle building project, the Lord commanded Moses to have the men who worked in the Tabernacle to each pay a half of shekel for a ransom for their souls. In God's system, the offering was of an equal portion and His justice prevailed. This is a key to a successful building project. No one could contribute more or less; the Lord had accommodated the rich and the poor. The half shekel was equivalent to a silver coin.

> *The rich shall not give more, and the poor give less than half a shekel, when they give an offering unto the Lord, to make an atonement for your souls. And you shall take the atonement money of the children of Israel, and shall appoint it for the service of the tabernacle of the congregation; that it may be a memorial unto the children of Israel before the Lord, to make atonement for your souls.*
> *(Exodus 30:11-16)*

A Place Reserved

According to the Justice of the Lord, there is a place reserved called a Lake of Fire. During one of Jesus teachings to His followers, He spoke of a parable of the wicked servant, and the result of his wickedness. The word declares, "It is appointed for men to die once, and after this, judgment" (Hebrews 9:27). There is a physical and a spiritual death that will occur in your life.

> *His lord was wroth, and delivered him to the tormentors, till he should pay all that was due unto him.*
> *(Matthew 18:32-34)*

> *They that feared the Lord spoke often to one another: and the Lord hearkened, and heard it, and a book of remembrance was written before Him for them that feared the Lord, and that thought upon His name.*
> *(Malachi 3:16)*

The scriptures tell us that in heaven there is a book of 'Remembrance.' This statement captures my curiosity about the reasons why some people will do the devil's dirty job? I often ask the question if there was a notification on a poster board that read, "HELP WANTED? Contact the Devil within." The rewards and the consequences of our actions should be checked. May the Lord help us! In the principles of the bible, it seems easy to identify that it was God's job to do the justice and judgment on behalf of His people.

    The Apostle John, in the Book of Revelation, had seen a vision which was about the after-death experience. He saw that there were books opened, and in it was written according to the records of men. He continued to say that God also had a special place reserved for the wicked, and a place for the righteous to reside forever. You can be mindful of your records in God's book, as it is your choice that matters.

God's Justice and Judgment

I saw the dead, small and great, stand before God; and the books were opened, and another book was opened, which is the book of life: and the dead were judged out of those things which were written in the books, according to their works. And whosoever was not found in the book of life was cast into the lake of fire.
(Revelation: 20:12-15)

In another reference, as Jesus taught the disciples, He validated these covenant words that say, "If you say you know Him, and don't keep His commandments, you are a liar, and the truth is not in you" (1 John 2:3-6). Those were harsh words, but Jesus was basically saying that in God's kingdom there will be no liars nor rebellious people.

To be sure that you know Him, you must allow the Holy Spirit to teach you how to become liken to His character of love and patience, and to walk and talk that which is pleasing in the sight of the Lord. The apostle Paul preached that the way to God's kingdom is love and he admonished the saints to understand that in the justice system of the Lord all it requires is for you not to owe no one anything, except to love – for it fulfills the law (Romans 13:8-10).

Paul admonished the believers, and he said that all the Law is fulfilled in one word, even in this: "Thou shall love thy neighbor as thyself" (Galatians 5:14). Paul told Timothy that the end of the commandment is charity out of a pure heart and a good conscience, and of sincere faith (1 Timothy 1:5).

It is essential for every believer to reconsider the love of God and to strive diligently to be in God's good books. The bible says that there is a book of remembrance written and the name of those that fear God will be recorded in it (Malachi

3:17). The Lord has promised to give you everlasting life, which begins the moment you accept Him into your heart. And through the sacrifice of His own life, you will live in His eternal presence forever and ever, Amen.

> *He (the Lord) had shown you, O man, what is good. What does the Lord require of you, but to act justly, to love mercy, and to walk humbly with your God.*
> *(Micah 6:8)*

Chapter 7
HIS AUTHORITY

Jesus is the first begotten of the Father and all authority belongs to Him. It can be said that Jesus was given the 'Power of Attorney' for life. The definition of a "power of attorney" is that it is a document given to someone to be used to make decisions on your behalf in their private affairs. This means the person received the authorization and they have a legal right to designate a call to action in some legal matters. This appointment can be immediately effective by the request of the other person.

The explanation has positioned our Lord and King with an unlimited authority and power. In the bible, John the Revelator had declared that the Lord appeared to him in a vision. He declared that His name was "Yahweh," which is the Hebrew interpretation of "YHVH." In English it is interpreted, "I AM, that I AM." The Lord used the phrase to reveal in the first person of the English language that "I will be, who I will be." He was the beginning and the end, and He is "the One who is, the One who was, and the One who is to Come." Jesus revealed that all authority belongs to Him in the present, in the past, and in the future (Revelation 1:8). In the days of Moses, he had encountered the Lord in all His splendor.

In Hebrew, God is called *Elohim*. This means that He is the Supreme Judge. The Hebrews sages say that this particular name of God is never used out of respect for the Almighty

God. The Israelites usually refer to God as the King of kings and Lord of lords. They recognize that the Lord has the supreme power and the right to determine what happens on the earth and in your life.

In reference to an earthly king, he has all possession and all the authority over his kingdom. It is obvious that this king must determine what goes on in his kingdom. He determines the punishable and pardonable laws of his kingdom. His jurisdiction gives him the right to acquit or pronounce judgment in each individual case. Also, in this kingdom he decides what will be permitted in the area of activities, such as sports, and for the availability of the types of food that would be accessible to the poor and the rich people. For instance, if they are of a religious group, the king's authority goes beyond comprehension. He can cultivate a system of injustice or righteous justice according to his decrees.

In the book of Esther there was the plot of the execution against the Jewish people. King Ahasuerus had given Haman the authority to destroy the people under Haman's deceitful plan. He devised a conspiracy to cause Mordecai to bow to a man. In the Jewish culture the people would not bow to any other gods, but the King of kings, and there was no mention of the Lord throughout the book of Esther. The Hebrew scholars say that the name, "Esther," means "to hide" in Hebrew. Here the Jews seemed to be hiding their identity in the story for they were captives of previous kings. However, the Lord of mercies saw their injustice and caused Haman's plans to backfire. The opposite occured as the Lord intercepted the authority of the king and gave his authority and favor to queen Esther and her uncle Mordecai that resulted in the destruction of Haman and his wicked family (Esther 3:12-13).

On one occasion in the parables, Jesus illustrated the authority in reference to the kingdom of Heaven. He gave an example of a certain king and the marriage of his son at the wedding feast. Jesus mentioned that the king had the authority to invite who he wished. Therefore, he sends invitation to those he thought would come to celebrate with him. And the bible says that they made no effort to attend. So, the king requested that his servants go out and gather as many as they could find, both good and bad. Then, his servants clothed them in wedding garments that the king had requested for the wedding party. However, there was one man who came to the wedding who was inappropriately dressed. Here, Jesus used the parallel to say that the King had all authority to cast the man out of the feast, and into the outer darkness (Matthew 22:1-13). In this story the sages say that the attire represented God's righteousness. Therefore, the man represents the one who wants to come to God in his own self-righteousness.

For we must all appear before the judgement seat of Christ; that everyone may receive the things done in his body, according to that he had done, whether it be good or bad.
(2 Corinthians 5:10)

In the kingdom of Heaven there is an identical operational system and the Lord Jesus has the authority to reject those who are not dressed in their armor of Righteousness. This is an analogy of the wedding feast in describing the sinner who does not repent. Throughout the bible, God's authority is eminent. In reading and studying the word of God, I was astonished to find that God has authoritative gifts and keys, and He uses these keys in His kingdom, and there are mystery keys. He has keys that He has distributed freely to those with whom He chooses. Then, there are those keys that He desires to keep for Himself.

The Mystery Keys

The Lord gives these special keys to whom He pleases!

1. **The Key of the House of David** – God gave *to* his servant Eliakim (Isaiah 22:20-23).

    In Hebrew language the name Eliakim means *"the One God will raise up as a Prophet like the Savior Jesus Christ."*

2. **The Keys of the gates of the Grave** – the Lord *had given to* Peter.

    The keys that were given to Peter authorized him to open doors. Peter, through his life and the revelation he received, has fulfilled the promises of the Lord for the Jews and Gentiles to do greater works.

    > *Jesus said, 'Thou art Peter, and upon this rock I will build my church; and the gates of the grave shall not prevail against it.*
    > *(Matthew 16:18-19)*

3. **The Key of Government** - The bible says that Jesus possesses all authority (Matthew 28:18). He has the power to open and shut any door against your life situations. These keys

are accessible to those who walk upright with the Lord Jesus Christ. John the Revelator had a vision of Christ that revealed that Jesus has all authority.

> 'These things said He that hath the Key of David, He that open, and no man shut, and shut and no man open.'
> (Revelation 3:7)

The Keys of the Lord

The Lord God possesses three mystery keys by Himself. These are revealed throughout the bible. They are *The Key to the Womb, the Key of Rain and the Key of the Grave*.

1. <u>**The Key to open the Womb.**</u>
The Bible says, "*And when God saw that Leah (Jacob's wife) was hated, <u>He opened her womb</u>*" (Genesis 29:31).

   In the case of Rachel, the Lord closed her womb because the bible says that she was hateful of her sister Leah. Rachel had a root of jealousy in her heart because of her father Laban; for he had tricked Jacob into marrying her sister Leah first. Then, Rachel became Jacob's wife after seven more years. Her dilemma made her become irritated and envious, and she blamed Jacob for not giving her children. But the bible says that Jacob interceded for Rachel, and the Lord, in His mercy, remembered Rachel and opened her womb (Genesis 30:22).

   The scriptures also reveal that God used this key to open the womb of many women to achieve His will upon the earth. The Lord visited Sarah, the wife of Abraham, and He opened her womb and she became the mother of Isaac in her old age (Genesis 21:1-6). Moreover, the Lord had shut the wombs of Abimelech's wife and the women servants, because he took Sarah into his place. After Sarah was returned to Abraham, he prayed unto the Lord and the Lord opened the womb of Abimelech's wife and women servants.

The Lord opened the womb of Elizabeth who was barren. The bible says that Elizabeth and her husband, Zachariah, were in advanced age when the angel visited her. She became the mother of John the Baptist who prepared the way for the Lord (Luke 1).

The Lord opened the womb of Hannah. She was barren and her dilemma was that her husband had children with another woman. She was intimidated by the other woman and was often sadden about her situation. But Hannah saw a need in the temple of God, for Eli was getting advanced in age and his son were not obedient to the Lord's work. Therefore, she changes her cries and decided to intercede for a prophet to do the work of the Lord. And the Lord answered her prayers and she received a son, and she called his name, Samuel. His name in Hebrew means, "God has heard." Samuel became the prophet that judged Israel for many years (I Samuel 2).

God had opened the womb of Samson's mother whose name was Hazelelponi (1 Chronicles 4:3). The bible says that the angel of the Lord appeared to the woman and said that she would conceive a special son; for she was childless. Her name in the Hebrew language means "the woman was one who saw the face of the angel." Samson was a Nazarite unto the Lord from the womb and he delivered Israel out of the hand of the Philistines (Judges 13).

Michal, the wife of king David and the daughter of king Saul, had the reverse occur. She had despised David for his radical praise to the Lord after his victory over the recovery of the Ark of the Covenant. David tried to reassure her of his actions, however, she called it disgraceful, and the Lord shut up her womb. As a result of her unwarranted discontentment, she died childless.

In this example of God's authority, it is revealed that the Lord is pleased with your individual style of worship. Therefore, Micah's behavior is a depiction of a disgruntle believer who becomes upset when another person has a radical praise towards the Lord. It tells us that the Lord marks the insensitivity towards a person's action of gratefulness for whatever reasons they experience a deliverance that has been overwhelming.

2. *<u>The Key for Rain</u>*
The Lord shall open unto thee his good treasure, the heaven to give the rain unto thy land in his season.
(Deuteronomy 28:12)

And it shall be, that whoso will not come up of all the families of the earth unto Jerusalem, to worship the King, the Lord of hosts, even upon them shall be no rain.
(Zachariah 14:17)

Moses was older now and he knew that it was time to rehearse the warning of the Lord's desire to the people before his departure. He cautioned the people and explained that it is the Lord who holds *the key of rain.*

God's Justice and Judgment

Take heed to yourselves, that your heart be not deceived, and turn aside, and serve other gods, and worship them; and then cause the Lord's wrath to be kindled against you, and He shut up the heaven, that there be no rain, and that the land yield not her fruit; less you perish quickly from off the good land which the Lord give you.
(Deuteronomy 11:16-17)

When heaven is shut up, and there is no rain, because they have sinned against you; if they pray towards this place, and confess your name, and turn from their sins, when you affect them.
(1 Kings 8:35)

Another proof of the Lord holding the key to rain was in King Solomon prayer. The bible says that at the dedication of the Tabernacle, king Solomon prayed and acknowledged that in their disobedience God will shut up the heaven and give them no rain.

On one occasion as the Lord appeared to King Solomon, He warned him in the dream saying, "If I (the Lord) shut up the heaven that there be no rain, or if I command the locusts to devour the land, or if I send the pestilence among the people. This will be because the people did not humble themselves and pray and seek my face; and turn from their wicked ways. Nevertheless, if they will repent, then the Lord will hear from heaven and will heal their land" (2 Chronicles 7:12-14).

Therefore, this means that some droughts are related to the disobedience of the people. For at their obedience to the Lord's commands, He sent the rain from the heaven.

The story of the prophet Elijah made it seem that he understood the principle of the Lord concerning the rain. He used the people's rebellion against God; for they had been worshippers of idolatry. He had made a decree according to Moses' words, and as a result, the Lord answered in judgment. According to Elijah's faith in the authority of God's judgment, the bible says that heaven was supernaturally shut up, and there was no rain, and the dew stopped falling upon the land for three years. In other words, there arose famine in the land, and in a famine, there is drought and scarcity of food (1 Kings 17:18).

3. **<u>The Key to the Grave</u>**
This key is significant to the resurrection from the dead. Only Jesus Christ died, and He got Himself up again through the supernatural power of resurrection. In the bible, only Jesus has the keys to Death and the Grave or Sheol. The word "Sheol" in the Hebrew language means for the specific place of burial that is known as "Hell."

> *I am He that lived, and was dead; and, behold, I am alive for evermore, Amen; and have the keys of hell and of death.*
> *(Revelation 1:18)*

> *And ye shall know that I am the Lord, when I have opened your graves, O my people, and brought you up out of your graves.*
> *(Ezekiel 37:13)*

During the ministry of Jesus, He walked in His authority to perform the miracle of raising people from the dead. Lazarus was a prime story of the supernatural power of raising someone from the dead. The bible says that it was after four days that

Lazarus was in the grave and could have already been in a state of the process of decomposition. Anyway, Jesus arrived on the scene and He commanded Lazarus to come forth. And at that very moment, Lazarus stood up and the miracle of resurrection happened before many witnesses (John 11:38-44). The scholars say that this resurrection miracle was a foreshadow of the fulfillment of Jesus Christ's own death and resurrection.

Another miracle was the story of the widow woman and the funeral procession for her son. As Jesus approached the city gate, He saw the mother weeping. Her circumstance was of excessive grief; for she was a widow, and now her only son was dead. Then, Jesus was full of compassion. He knew her situation and came near and touched the brier. Those that were carrying the dead boy stood still. Then Jesus commanded the young man to "Arise!" and instantly, the boy sat up and began to speak. This meant that supernaturally the young man was resurrected from the dead and then delivered to his mother. After the miracle, the bible says that the people began to fear, and they glorified God (Luke 7:12-16).

The Decree to Live!

Is it rational to say that, the Lord has the authority to decree that you shall live and not die?

In the time of Jesus' ministry, the apostle Luke was a physician by profession. All his writings are testimonies from a medical point of view. He basically detailed the miracles of Jesus. His records are captivating, because he recognized the great authority by which Jesus Christ operated and he proclaimed that Jesus had a supernatural lifestyle. From Luke's point of view, he saw that Jesus' ministry towards the people was of healing and deliverance to the sick and those oppressed of the devil.

In Matthew's account of Jesus, there was much emphasis on the supernatural authority, and the effects that Jesus had over the events of His death and His resurrection. Matthew's desire for details was in the elaborated version of Christ's crucifixion. He told of the many supernatural signs on the evening when Jesus Christ gave up the ghost (or died). He spoke of the reaction of nature; for at that very moment the sun turned black and there was an earthquake where the rocks broke apart. He also said that the veil of the tabernacle was torn in two from top to bottom at the same time. In addition, the sages say that the Menorah or the candle stick center light never kept light again, and the doors of the tabernacle opened on their own accord, which was impossible before. The door Solomon built needed about twelve strong men to open them and close them again.

After the resurrection of Jesus, Matthew said that the graves of dead saints were opened and many of the saints arose and came out of their graves and walked the streets of the city where many people saw them (Matthew 27:51-53). And according to the apostle Luke, he said that the saints went into the Holy City, Jerusalem, appearing to many of the people.

These reports have esteemed the power of God and have the notion of encouragement that says it is only Jesus Christ that has the final say! The devil does not have the final say. There is a song that I have heard with the lyrics of these word, and it does have some gratification of truth. In my weird imagination, I wondered if the people who saw Jesus performing many miracles had sang this declaration of praise.

Could you imagine brother Job? He must have had

this revelation too, as he faced his many trials. The result was awesome. How about king David? Throughout his life, he had experienced the hand of the Lord in his situations, whether they were for good or bad. In his writings of the Psalms, he has proven that he understood that Jesus has the final say. The bible noted that David was always penitent, and he continued in the faith until his last day.

Make haste, O God, to deliver me; make haste to rescue me, O Lord. Let them be ashamed and confounded that seek after my soul: let them be confused, and put to confusion, that desire my hurt.
(Psalm 70:1-2)

Chapter 8
HIS PASSION FOR LIFE

And He will be the stability of your times, and strength of your salvation: for the fear of the Lord is your treasure.
(Isaiah 33:6)

God's desire is for you to live in His presence eternally. He wants you to have life and have it more abundantly and to experience His presence (John 10:10).

In the garden of Eden, God's glorious presence was available to man until the time of Adam's fall. In His compassion for human life, God's original plan was to restore mankind back to an awesome fellowship with Him. One preacher explained it simply by saying that God wanted a family and created you and I for that purpose. The bible says that when God called Abraham to become the father of a nation, He wanted relationship and a people to commune with Him. Then, the Lord God made a covenant promise with Abraham that He would establish his generations to be called children of God. The Lord chose the Hebrew children and He desired to expedite his Glory in their lives, that they might experience the blessings of His promises.

In those days, Abraham, Isaac and Jacob chose to trust the Lord and walk in His command. The Lord sought ways to lead His people into righteous living, however, sin was still prevalent around their land and some of the people brazenly sinned and rejected God. Even though the Lord spoke through His prophets and pleaded with the people; they refused to return to lives that would be pleasing in the sight of God. Hence, the nation was judged, and they began to experience a series of destructive events as they wandered in the wilderness. The experience in Egypt should have convinced them that God loves life and His desire was for them to enter their Promised Land.

Their journey to Canaan should have taken a few days, but instead their journey lasted forty years. Jewish people were rebellious to the Lord and they rebellion causing them to murmur and complain consistently; they soon forgot what the Lord had done for them. This characteristic of the human behavior tends to reflect to those who have an ungrateful attitude, and this lead to doubt and unbelief. The children of Israel seemed divided in their faith towards the Lord. It had produced rebellion and evil workings as a result of their state of mind.

The Lord's passion for life caused Him to have compassion on the younger generations and in His mercy, He remembered His covenant with their father Abraham and in His mercy, He chose to deliver them at a set time. This event is usually celebrated as a Memorial Day at Passover. The history of Moses and how his journey prepared him to become their deliverer at the age of eighty years old has the similarity of a path like Jesus Christ, because Moses had gone through his wilderness experiences also for forty years. Therefore, when the Lord called Moses, He gave him a platform to operate in the miraculous on His behalf to free the Hebrew children.

The people operated in rebellion and had influenced others to commit sins and rebellion against the Lord (Exodus

12:38). The bible tells us that some of the people of Egypt had come along with the Jews, because they were afraid of the plagues. Could they have an influential factor in the Hebrews' lives? I seriously doubt if the people would have seen the miracles and turned to the Lord wholeheartedly. The other thing to consider is that these people had blended in among them, and they did not believe in the God of Abraham, Isaac and Jacob.

A mixed multitude went up also with them; and flocks, and herds.
(Exodus 12:38)

The Lord is passionate to operate in His plan for your life like the children of Israel. Yet, there might be those friends and family members who are not passionate about what the Lord is doing in your life. It is very important to consider who is on board in your camp, as the Lord is taking you somewhere.

The Lord desires to have a personal encounter with His people, and He wants to anoint everyone to become a kingdom of priests and a holy nation. In the bible there was an event where the Lord commanded Moses to prepare the people for a visitation with Him. To be prepared, they had to be washed and cleansed for that special day. As the people gathered at the bottom of the mount, they suddenly heard the voice of the Lord sounding like thunders and lightnings. Hence, they became afraid, and they told Moses to go up and speak to God, then come down and tell them all that He said.

It is because of fear that the average human being is not interested in having an encounter with the Lord. I am sure I would have desired to hear the Lord for myself. This is a mistake, and today, we are still refusing to hear God for ourselves. The Lord's passion was for the Israelites to have a face-to-face encounter with Him. The Hebrew scholar says that they just wanted His hand (which represents the blessings of material things). Could it be that this is the very reason why God had put the statutes and laws in place to guide them in the ways of life; in order to curb their selfish ambitions? (Exodus 19)

The God of Love!

The Lord is a God of Love! The bible has exemplified that the Lord is preferential in portraying a social model that illuminates His likes and dislikes; or basically the things He loves and hates.

Similarly, as you reflect on your emotions, it is obvious that you do show love and at other times express hatred. Hence, in your happiest times you portray joy, and there is a positive look of a lovely countenance. In the event of you becoming upset, your mood of behavior would convert to a very rude or intolerable personality. It is very uncomfortable to be around a person in a conflicted personality.

It seems very easy to fall in love, but it seems much easier to fall out of love. It results into hate or despise for each party to adjust to their positions. We all experience such emotions from time to time regardless who we are.

It is said that we were made in God's image and likeness. Do you think the Lord can have a similar personality?

The Hebrew scholars says that it is believed that the Lord God also has two sides and two faces. Their conclusion was derived from the fact that in the Hebrew language there is no word for *face*. In the scriptures the word used is, *"paniym"* and in Hebrew it means "faces."

This theory indicates that mankind also has two faces and he can operate in two behavioral patterns. There is the possibility that mankind is inclined to be a good or an evil person. I found this information fascinating, and a contentious statement at the same time.

There is another theory for the meaning of the word *paniym*. It is said, *"What is on your face is a sign of what is in your heart inside."* This statement to some degree was derivative of the thought process that requires some type of imagination.

On the final days of Moses, he was celebrating his birthday of the one hundred and twentieth year. As he stood up and spoke the 'Song of Moses,' he spoke it in the hearing of the people and proclaimed, "How great is the Lord." Moses was confirming that God is loving and that He will make a way for His children. He went on to ascribe and declare the Lord's reputation of mercy and compassion. He reminded them that the Lord is perfect in His way of judgment, and that, He is a God of truth and righteous justice (Deuteronomy 32:3-4).

> *I will publish the name of the Lord: Proclaim your greatness to our God. He is the Rock, His work is perfect: for all His ways are judgement: a God of truth and right justice.*
> (Deuteronomy 32:3-4)

King David quoted the song of Moses when he sang of the goodness and the love of the Lord his God (2 Samuel 22:1-4).

In the book of Revelation, John the Revelator says that we will sing the song of Moses in heaven (Revelation 15:3-4). This means that we will all sing of His love, compassion and mercy to all the saints.

We read in the book of Isaiah chapter 66 where the prophet had prophesied that the Lord's justice prevailed in love for His people. His judgment was a result of their rebellious attitude, and in their repentance, He did turn back to love. God had put them out of the land, to bring them in again, and He has promise to restore them in His love.

The analogy of the prophet Isaiah was that of when Israel turn to their Father God, and His son Jesus Christ, then the Lord shall prevail over Jerusalem in His mercy, and in His justice and judgment (Isaiah 66:11-13). In other words, the scripture has a simple clarification of the promise of the Lord God and they are relevant to every believer today.

1. God loves you.
2. God hugs and kisses.
3. God lets you sit on His lap.
4. God will comfort and protect you (like a mother covers her children).

Things God Hates

God is holy! In Him there is no unrighteousness. The scriptures declare precisely that <u>God hates every sin.</u> Some people often say that God is a compassionate and longsuffering towards the sinners, therefore, He will always forgive your sins.

The Lord told Zephaniah that there will be a day of judgment, and He would search the city light with a candle, and punish the men that are unconcerned, that say in their heart, "The Lord will not do good, neither evil to them" (Zephaniah 1:3).

Let me make a clarification: The Lord really does not hate the sinner, but the sins they constantly practice. At the top of the list is the sin of murmuring and complaining, then the spirits of abominations, and the spirit of blaspheming or cursing and profanity.

The Spirit of Blaspheming
Concerning the spirit of blaspheming, it is inclusive of blasphemy against the Holy Ghost and it is unforgivable. A definition for blaspheming is an act of offense which is against someone for the purpose of disrespect, and it results in a type of cursing or swearing. The number of times the word was used in the bible is about fourteen times. According to the story of Peter, when he denied the Lord Jesus Christ at the trial, it was said that he had used profanity to avoid the people from exposing who he really was. It was his way of distracting attention from him being one of the disciples that walked with Jesus.

Blaspheming was a serious crime to the Lord and He had made it known to Moses, "A man that blasphemes the name of the Lord is cursed." There was a son of an Israelite woman, but his father was an Egyptian and he was a grandson of the Dan tribe. He had blasphemed the name of the Lord and the people brought him to Moses and they made him a prisoner. Then the Lord spoke to Moses and instructed him to put this man outside the camp and let the congregation stone him; it was to be a lesson to the others (Leviticus 24:10-16).

The Spirit of Murmuring
The definition for murmuring is to mutter complaints. Moreover, no complaining and murmuring give God glory. It will result in you becoming rebellious against the Lord, and you will forget all the good things the Lord has done for you. Murmuring can deteriorate your faith in the Lord's promises also. This will give the devil an opportunity to speak his lies to you which can result in unbelief. The scriptures make it clear that the Lord hates murmuring.

> *The foolishness of man pervert his ways: and his heart fret against the Lord.*
> *(Proverb 19:3)*

The sins of murmuring and complaining were reiterated as the key issue the Lord had with the children of Israel throughout the bible. The Lord, in many situations, demonstrated His disapproval of this type of behavior. From the days that the Lord delivered the children of Israel out of Egypt, they had somehow forgotten all that He had done for them and they murmured and complained constantly.

Throughout their journey, Moses became fed up with the people, as they continually murmured and complained against the Lord. It made him lose his temper and caused him to smite the rock twice. This disqualified Moses from entering the land of promise. I could sympathize with Moses, because people are the most difficult beings to lead. At times, the Lord also was disgusted with the people. He asked Moses and Aaron, "How long will this wicked assembly keep complaining about me?" (Numbers 14:26-30)

All the congregation lifted their voice and cried, and

the people wept that night. And all the children murmured against Moses and Aaron. They said unto them, "Would God that we died in the Land of Egypt! Or would God we had died in the wilderness" (Numbers 14:1-2). The main reason for the Israelites murmuring was that they craved for the foods of Egypt. The Lord was so angry that He rained down meat and it caused many to die in their lust (Numbers 11:4-10). They portrayed the signs of an ungrateful heart.

In those days, when Jesus walked upon the earth the people murmured much, as the bible says that they were of two opinions concerning his Lordship and so they murmured amongst themselves (John 7:11-13). In any event, because of their murmurings, the chief priest sent officers to take Jesus, but he escaped.

In the book of Jude, the apostle explained the ungodly characters amongst the people who were responsible for the death of the Messiah. They were those that can be identified by their speech against the Lord. He declares that these are murmurers, complainers, those walking after their own lusts, and their mouths speaking grumbling words constantly (Jude 1:16).

The Spirit of Abominations
Scriptures say that there are some sins which God never pardons. In the list below, there are sins that God calls abominations (Proverbs 6:16-19). Abominable sins are those intentional acts of sin that people do to the Lord and to other people, that the Lord despises or disapproves.

> *These six things do the Lord Hate: Yes, seven are an abomination unto him: A proud look a lying tongue,*

and hands that shed innocent blood, a heart that devise wicked imaginations, feet that be swift in running to mischief, a false witness that speak lies, and he that sow discord among the brethren.
(Proverbs 6:16-19)

1. <u>A Proud Look:</u> A person that loves himself and hates God, and he who lives an evil lifestyle. These persons will not see the face of God without true repentance.
2. <u>A Lying tongue:</u> The lying tongue is an intentional act of violation to truth. A lying tongue can destroy the effectiveness of another person's life.
3. <u>Hands that shed innocent blood:</u> This means anyone who maliciously takes another man's life. Taking the life of the child is another way of shedding innocent blood.
4. <u>A heart that devise wickedness:</u> The wicked imagination of every evil thought and plan against God and Man, and these people continue in their schemes of wickedness and rebellion.
5. <u>Feet that be swift in running to mischief</u>: Those that are swift to mischief, and their hearts feel like they are rejected of the Lord.
6. <u>A false witness that speaks Lies:</u> One that bears false witness against their neighbor. They continually carry gossip which has no merit.
7. <u>He that sow discord among the brethren:</u> Those that love to cause division and strife through malicious gossip and opinions for their own selfish ambitions.

The bible is explicit about the sins that the Lord hates and disapproves. Throughout the scriptures, they are the characteristics of those who have shown their operations in these types of sins. As you go through with the list, some of these attitudes must be eliminated from the believer's life. The Lord mentioned all these things in the His word to give us an understanding of His standards for you!

The Lord hates false accusations. There is a law for bearing false news to cause the innocent to be penalized already in place in the days of Moses. The Lord told Moses that the people should not bear the sin of spreading fasle reports, "Fake news" was eident in the book of Exodus (Exodus 23:1-2)

The Wicked Heart
The story is told of a descendant of Amalek whose name was Haman. His heart was wicked. He plotted for the destruction of the Jewish people, but the Lord – even though His name was never mentioned in this story – was the judge of this matter (Esther 5:14).

A Proud Spirit
A proud spirit is found in the case of the Egyptian Pharaoh who experienced the Exodus of the Children of Israel. His pride caused him to be rebellious as he refused to let the children of Israel go. The Lord God had many bouts with Pharaoh and as a result he surrendered after the final plague that caused the death of his firstborn son.

A Lying Tongue

Ananias and Sapphira operated in a *lying tongue*. They told Peter an untruth about their business transaction. It wasn't even necessary, because the offerings were free willed, but they wanted to impress the others maybe (Acts 5:1-11).

> *Lying lips are abomination to the Lord: but they that deal truly are his delight.*
> *(Proverb 12:22)*

Swift to Mischief

The story of Gehazi is a story of a man who was *swift to mischief*. His mischief became his downfall. He had a spirit of covetousness and when he knew that Elisha refused to take any offerings from Naaman, he ran after him and requested talents of silver and changes of garments from his hand. His reward for covetousness was Naaman's leprosy (2 Kings 5:22-27).

Hands that Shed Innocent Blood

Cain committed *the sin of murder* against his brother Abel. The bible tells us that he was *jealous* of his brother's offering, and he deliberately shed innocent blood when he killed Abel. This act of sin is prevalent today in families, and in the church (Genesis 4:8).

The hearts of the people before the flood had *devised wickedness* in the earth. The bible declared that the Lord was repentant that he had created them.

> *And God saw that the wickedness of man was great in the earth, and that every imagination of the thoughts*

> *of his heart was only evil continually. And it repented the Lord that he had made man on the earth.*
> *(Genesis 6:5-6)*

False teachers
There are those preachers and prophets who operate in rebellion, pretending to speak the truth against the word of God. These made others follow in their ways and through covetousness receive things from the people to promote their own agendas (2 Peter 2:1- 4).

> *A false witness shall not be unpunished, and he that speak lies shall not escape.*
> *(Proverb 19:5)*

The apostle John has an awesome explanation that if God did not spare the angels that sinned, but casted them out and down into hell, delivering them unto chains of darkness to be reserved unto judgment. Therefore, the Lord will severely punish those walking in rebellion against the Word of God. There was a list of offenses given to consider in (Revelation 21:18).

> *The fearful and unbelieving, and the abominable, and murderers, and whoremongers, and sorcerers, and idolaters, and <u>all liars</u>, shall have their part in the lake which burn with fire and brimstones: which is the second death.*
> *(Revelation 21:8)*

These people would experience a sudden calamity, and they would be broken suddenly without remedy. My prayer is this would never be your portion, as the bible declares that His commandments are not grievous to those who believe.

> *By this we know that we love the children of God, when we love God, and keep his commandments, for this is the Love of God, that we keep his commandments: and his commandments are not grievous.*
> *(1 John 5:2-3)*

It is only the Lord God who can renew the evil heart of man. He laid down His life as a sacrifice, and through His blood, you can experience new life and encounters with the Holy Ghost and the grace of God.

> *A new heart also will I give you, a new spirit will I put within you: and I will take away the stony heart out of your flesh, and I will give you a heart of flesh.*
> *(Ezekiel 36:26)*

The Separation

Jesus was teaching the people about the parable story of the talents. He continued to tell another story in relation to the Son of man and the King, as He explained the position of the glory, and all the holy angels coming down from heaven. Jesus, in His speech, told them of the nations, and how they were separated into groups. He referred to them as shepherds and their animals, where there were sheep and goats. Jesus said that the sheep stood on the right hand and the goats on the left.

Jesus explains a scenario and the outlook of the pleasure of the king, and what made him displeased. The concept of the sheep and the goats were used in reference to the good and bad things people do. The bible declared that the king then blessed those who were righteous with honor, and those that were not with curses.

> *Then He will say to those on His left hand, "Depart from Me, you cursed, into everlasting fire, prepared for the devil and his angels.*
> *(Matthew 25:31-41)*

The very concept of the Lord's judgment in a person's life is inexplicable. There were many stories in the scriptures which declared that there was much wickedness before the Lord, and about the outcome of such wickedness. According to the book of Ezekiel, the Lord had chosen Israel as His peculiar people, yet they chose to rebel in their wickedness against the Lord. They never understood the concept of holiness and He spoke through the prophets and pleaded for them to return to Him. However, they chose to rebel, and they began continually to be judged and many lost their lives.

> *"Say to them, As I live!" declares the Lord God, "I take no pleasure in the death of the wicked, but rather that the wicked turn from his way and Turn back, turn back from your evil ways! Why then would you die, O house of Israel.*
> *(Ezekiel 33:11)*

The Lord is also asking you and I to turn away from every wickedness that would interfere with His blessings and compassion in our lives. The scripture says that if the wicked shall turn from his wickedness and do that which is lawful and right, he shall live out his days. One example is King David, he is an inspiration, and he represents the figure of humanity and repentance. In his weakness, he turned from his wicked acts back to the Lord. Then, there was King Saul, who did not repent and turn from his errors. And the judgment of the Lord fell upon him. He might have spared Jonathan's life, maybe, if he had repented and began to obey the commands of the Lord. This is a teachable moment. As centuries went by and many evil people according to the Lord, did not live out their days. There is a similar behavior pattern in the world today.

    Many of the prophets had lost their lives over periods of time after they had entered the Promise Land. They were living among the children of God and they kept warning the people of the consequences of their disobedience. Throughout the bible there is the pattern of a roller coaster lifestyle of the people. They would repent for a little while, and then, they would be turning their backs on God and practice sin. The atrocities of the people should have been lessons for another generation, but sadly they chose to constantly live separated from God. Because of their lifestyle of sin and wickedness, there are a few judgments found in the bible that reference the declaration that the Lord proclaimed over the people.

> *I will punish the world for their evil, and the wicked for their iniquity; and I will cause the arrogancy of the proud to cease, and will lay low the haughtiness of the ruthless.*
> *(Isaiah 13:11)*

Woe unto the wicked! It shall be ill with him: for the reward of his hand shall be given to Him.
(Isaiah 3:11)

The soul that sin, it shall die. The Sons shall not bear the iniquity of the father, neither shall the father bear the iniquity of the son: The righteousness of the righteous shall be upon him, and the wickedness of the wicked shall be upon him.
(Ezekiel 18:20)

Chapter 9
THE CAPTAIN OF HOSTS

The Lord shall fight for you, ye shall hold your peace.
(Exodus 14:14)

This title of the Lord God was mentioned about 270 times in the scriptures. *The captain of hosts* was frequently used as a term that accentuated the capacity of strength and force that the Lord used in His authority and power.

In the book of John, chapter 20, the bible tells us that after the death of Jesus, the disciples were very afraid of the leaders who condemned Him. They had gone back to the place Jesus told them to wait and closed the door. However, on the first day of that week, Jesus appeared to them after He had resurrected. On that day, Jesus defiled the doors, for He found a way to come in unto them. As He appeared, He blessed them by saying "Peace be unto you." Jesus exercised His authority as He was not subjected to their lock door. Therefore, He is not subjected to your locked doors, in any area of your life.

The Lord had told Moses that he should not walk in fear. The bible declares that the Lord Himself will fight for you (Deuteronomy 3:22). The Lord had revealed His warrior nature to Moses and in the book of Exodus as He performed His glorious power against Pharaoh's army as a man of war.

Then sang Moses and the children of Israel this song unto the Lord, saying, "I will sing unto the Lord, for He has triumphed gloriously: The horse and his rider has He thrown into the sea."
(Exodus 15:1)

In another scripture, King David recognized the Lord was powerful as he asked the question (The Lord's distinctive warrior attitude was never confronted at any moment by anyone):

"Who is this King of glory?
He is the King of glory, the Lord of hosts."
(Psalms 24:8)

The scriptures declare that Jesus cleansed the tabernacle with a scourge of small cords, and He drove them out. This meant that there was some amount of fear for God within them and that they knew the words of God, therefore, they could not react to Jesus as He performed the cleansing act of His tabernacle.

    In my rechecking of the case of Adam versus the Lord, there is evidence written which indicates that the Lord and Adam had many walks and talks in the Garden of Eden. He knew of God's request to leave that particular tree alone, as the conversation of the forbidden tree was one of them. However, Adam failed to caution Eve on that day of temptation. Because of his unfaithful actions to God, it caused him to be driven out of the Garden of Eden. Then the Lord placed two of His warrior angels called "cherubim" to prevent them from entering in again.

    Jesus is the Chief and Captain of Hosts in His angel army. Throughout the scriptures, it is declared that His army of angels are armed and equipped to fight and protect those who Jesus calls His own. They represent the Lord in the natural and supernatural realms, as they work around the clock at His beckoning. The Lord give His angels charge over those that are bought with a price and washed in the blood of Jesus Christ (Psalms 91).

Bless the Lord, ye his angels, that excel in strength, that do His commandments, hearkening unto the voice of the Lord.
(Psalm 103:21)

He is a Mighty Warrior

One revelation that I saw was notable in the Bible is: *'Jesus has no fear in Him!'* It is a thought that will produce confidence in your faith walk.

I heard someone articulate a title in this terminology for the Lord Jesus, as they said that Jesus is the undisputed Heavy Weight Champion. He is like a boxer, pound for pound, as He has never lost a fight. It works great with my imagination, as I love boxing. Amen!

As the Messiah, Jesus is described as a Warrior-King who possessed a glittering sword in His hand. He renders vengeance to His enemies (Deuteronomy 32:41). He also uses His scepter to defend His people from their adversaries. The prophet Isaiah received the revelation of the Lord restoring Zion. It was there where he declares that it is the Lord Jesus who will come in His power and might to save His people.

> *Who is this that cometh from Edom, with dyed garments from Bozrah? This that is glorious in his apparel, travelling in greatness of his strength? I that speak in righteousness, mighty to save.* [This is 'Yeshua'- Jesus defeating his enemies.]
> *(Isaiah 63:1)*

John, in the book of Revelation, gave his account as he saw the Lord Jesus as He appeared to him in a warrior nature. He saw someone that nobody will mingle with. Not the devil, not Jezebel, not any type of sickness nor your enemies. As Judge and a Warrior, He wins His battles with such might and power every time. To put it into my perspective, the Lord flows with deliverance and healing in His wings.

> *I saw heaven opened, and behold a white horse; and he sat upon him was called Faithful and True, and in righteousness he Do judge and make war. His eyes were as a flame of fire, and on his head were many crowns; and he had a name written, that no man knew, but he himself.*
> *(Revelation 19: 11-16)*

King David recognized that in every battle he had ever fought, the Lord of Host was with him. Throughout history, King David was also declared as a mighty man of war. He had slain tens of thousands. His zealousness was as a conqueror for the children of Israel, as He won battles victoriously with the help of the Lord. For instance, one incident of the Philistines, as the story was told of the people being afraid of the giant Goliath threatening their existence. As David showed no fear, and boldly approached the enemy. Then he acknowledged who God was to him.

> *Then said David to the Philistine, you come to me with a sword, and with a spear, and with a shield: but I come to you in the name of the Lord of Hosts, the God of the armies of Israel.*
> *(1 Samuel 17:45–47)*

The bible declared that the Lord revealed Himself to Joshua. He experienced a vision of the Lord of Hosts, face-to-face. This incident happened as Joshua was by the city Jericho. Joshua was about to possess the Promise Land, as the Lord spoke and gave him the strategy of how they were to overthrow his enemies (Joshua 5:13-15).

At this season the children of Israel had not too long ago been circumcised by Joshua. The Lord knew that they were not in the best of health to battle, so He strategized a plan. The Lord instructed Joshua to let the priest and the people walk around the walls of Jericho for seven days. And on the seventh day, the people must walk around seven times with the blowing of the trumpets and a great shout. He supernaturally intervened and gave them the victory. (Joshua 6)

There are testimonies recorded in the word of God of many situations in which the Lord fought battles for His people. There was a time at Gibeon, when Lord delivered Joshua and the children of Israel with a great slaughter. He had chased the five kings and their armies along the way that went up to Beth-horon into an ambush. Then the Lord cast down stones from heaven upon them and they died instantly. The scriptures declare that there were more who died from the hailstones than they whom the children of Israel slew with the sword (Joshua 10: 8-14).

In the case of Hannah, the plight of being barren was so humiliating because Peninnah on the other hand had children. This story sounded similar to Rachel and Leah. It shows the different attitude of Hannah to Rachel, who accused Isaac of not giving her children. As Hannah acknowledged that He is the Lord of Host, she, by revelation, knew that He would fight for her in the uncomfortable situation.

As she aligned herself with the Lord by faith, and she recognized the need for a service in His tabernacle, Hannah changed her prayer, as she asks the Lord to bless her with a boy child for the service of His work. Hannah recognized the need of her contribution to the service to the Lord's house. As the bible says that Eli the priest was getting old and his sons were not fit for God's service. And the Lord exercised His authority to the injustice of Hannah's life. And Hannah fulfilled her vow as the child was weaned.

> *'O Lord of Hosts, if you will look on your handmaiden, and remember me, and give your hand maid a man child, then I will give him back to you all the days of his life. This is my vow.'*
> *(1 Samuel 1:11)*

These are exciting times for you to be living in as you can experience the Lord of Hosts in your life and circumstances. There are times when spiritually you are challenged as church becomes as usual, basically three songs, a scripture and the offerings, and you often wonder if the Lord can fix the situation. I am a living testimony and I know He will as you realign yourself. You recognize His need of you.

I have seen cases where there is the nature of sin that sometimes causes stubbornness, and the soul and body struggle to surrender to God's will. However, Jesus is merciful and He fights your battle so that you can be free to accomplish His plan for your life.

Today, it doesn't matter what the situation is. He will fight for you if you call upon His name. God will give His angels charge over you and help you to overcome. The Father did help his son Jesus in His time of troubles when He walked upon this earth.

> *He will give His angels charge over you, to keep you in all your ways.*
> *(Psalms 91:11)*

> *God has not given us a spirit of Fear, but of power and love and a sound mind.*
> *(2 Timothy 1:7)*

The Lord has a legacy of a victorious King. Jesus, as the Son of David, is all powerful. As you invite the Lord Jesus into your battles, you can be confident that your enemies will be defeated, every time. You need not entertain fear, as you know that He will fight for you as you put your trust in Him.

> *The Lord is with me as a mighty terrible one: therefore, my persecutors shall stumble, and they shall not prevail: they shall be greatly ashamed; for they shall not prosper: their everlasting confusion shall never be forgotten.*
> *(Jeremiah 20:11)*

Chapter 10
GOD IS INTENTIONAL

The Lord thy God in the midst of thee is mighty; he will save, he will rejoice over thee with joy; he will rest in his love, he will joy over thee with singing.
(Zephaniah 3:17)

The Lord intentionally waited in His Love, over four hundred and thirty years, and rescued baby Moses to a set him apart for Israel's deliverance. The scriptures say that Moses grew and was matured in Pharaoh's household to become familiar to the Egyptian lifestyle. Eventually, the Lord allowed some circumstances to occur in Moses' life that caused him to retrieve outside his comfort zone, and into the wilderness. In this story it seems like the Lord was resting in His love until the desire to create a deliverer was accomplished.

The children of Israel had found themselves in bondage as a result of their rebellious practices against the Lord. However, God in His mercy, had a planned time and season for their deliverance from slavery. The bible declares that He heard their cries and was moved with compassion. The Lord God looked down from heaven and saw their troubles. Therefore, the Lord had set out to rescue them from their afflictions and chose Moses for the mission. According to the Jewish calendar, the people celebrate a specific season called, "the Passover," in remembrance of God's execution of their Exodus from Egypt (Exodus 8-12).

The Lord had intentionally strengthened the Pharaoh of Egypt. The Pharaoh was described as a hardhearted man. Their people were characterized as pagans who worshiped many gods. According to the sages, the whole event looked like a boxing match as the Lord gave the Pharaoh punches, in the form of plagues. Yet he refused to give up until the Lord administered the final blow of death to every Egyptian firstborn. God knew the Egyptian culture and beliefs, and every plague was significant towards their worship. He intentionally pronounced judgment to reveal His authority as the Creator of the earth.

The tenth plague was the death of the firstborn. The Lord instructed Moses to have the Israelites slaughter a lamb and place the blood over their door posts. This act was to prevent the death angel from coming into their homes. The symbol of the lamb was deliberately chosen as their sacrifice for their deliverance, because it was a representation of a deity to the Egyptians called Khnum, which was the sign of a god of fertility or fruitfulness.

In the land of Egypt, the Israelites had practiced the abominable things as they also worshiped the Egyptian gods. Consequently, the Lord redeemed the Israelites the same hour of their grief. The Egyptians would do nothing to harm them since they were more focused on burying their dead loved ones. The Hebrew children were led out of Egypt with the intention that they would separate themselves from the pagan culture. God intended that they would live as His treasure in the light of His love.

The Lord Jesus Christ intended to let the believer come out of an evil culture and not partake of the sins of this world in order to not receive the plagues of sin (Revelation 18:4). Paul admonished, "Come out from among them, and be separate," (2 Corinthians 6:17) said the Lord, "and touch not the forbidden thing." This phrase simply means that, you should leave the things that are not pleasing to the Lord behind, and you should walk in the newness of the life through Jesus Christ.

Another God-intentional story was that of Joseph. He was sold into slavery by his brothers' hands. The Lord had permitted Joseph's demise so that His purposes could be fulfilled for the future of the Israelites. Joseph going into captivity was not accident. The Lord had prepared the season and the set time for his deliverance. Even though it was not always pleasant for Joseph, these events positioned him in Egypt to become a deliverer to help his father, Jacob, and his siblings in the time of famine. The sages say that Joseph's life was a type and foreshadow of Jesus Christ.

As for you, you thought evil against me; but God meant it for good, to bring to pass, as it is this day, to save much people alive.
(Genesis 50:20)

In the book of Samuel, it is revealed that the Lord was intentional in his judgment of Israel. King David had inquired of the Lord concerning the famine in Israel. The land had suffered for three years. It was the third year of the famine when David sought the Lord. Then the Lord answered David and said that the reason for the extended famine was because justice was not met for the Gibeonites. King Saul and his bloody house (as the Lord put it) was not yet judged.

The question is, "Who are the Gibeonites?" The scripture says that they were not children of Israel, but they were a remnant of the Amorites. These were the Gibeonites who disguised themselves as ambassadors and made a covenant with Joshua (Joshua 9:4-6). At that particular time, the children of Israel had not consulted the Lord concerning making an agreement with the Gibeonites. Therefore, once the agreement was made, it stood as an actual agreement in the sight of the Lord. Once Joshua finally realized that they were tricked, they allowed the Gibeonites to serve them as woodcutters and water fetchers for the assembly.

Years later, King Saul violated the treaty and murdered the Gibeonites. During the time that David became king there was a famine in Israel. According to the words of Moses, famine represents judgment from the Lord. Therefore, David knowing what the Lord said, decided to appease the Gibeonites. He inquired of them what they desired and they requested the heads of Saul's household.

Subsequently, David allowed the Gibeonites to put to death the seven sons of Saul (2 Samuel 21). The bible also says that God healed the land afterwards. In this short story, the lesson learned was that the Lord is faithful and requires faithfulness in covenant. Therefore, breaking treaty is a serious thing with God. It was also important before making decisions to consult with God.

The Lord was intentional when He anointed David as the king of Israel. David was spoken of many years through prophecy concerning his kingship when he was just a shepherd boy. David's training included many wilderness experiences, lions, bears and giants. Then, the Lord waited until his maturity for the role and set in motion the revoking of king Saul's throne.

God is Intentional

The mistakes David made during his reign caused him to experience the judgment of the Lord personally. The Lord caused David to lose his son that was produced by an affair; this was part of the judgment against his horrific sin. The horrible thing David did was immorality with Bathsheba, and his intentional death of her husband Uriah caused him many trials.

Through David's repentance, the Lord forgave him of his great sins and allowed him to live long enough to accumulate much of the wealth of gold and silver for the building of the temple. King David had the desire to build a house for the Lord. Thus, the Lord intentionally gave to David and the union of Bathsheba another son. He promised David that his son Solomon would build the temple in his stead (I Kings 5-6).

During the building project, Solomon was given the accumulation of gold and silver that David had stored up for the temple. Then Solomon sought help of a Gentile king to give him the timber for the temple. Therefore, the Lord intentionally allowed King Solomon and the Gentile king, Tyre, to come together to do the work of the Lord's house. In those days, this was a rare occurrence; and the scholars say that it was a foreshadow of the Jews and Gentiles becoming one in the faith to build God's kingdom.

> *And we know that all things work together for good to them that love God, to them who are called according in his purpose.*
> *(Romans 8:28)*

Jesus' Life was Intentional

From the foundation of the world, God's intention was to send a Savior into the world to deliver man from their sins. At the appointed time, the angel of God visited a righteous virgin name, Mary, and told her that she was chosen to carry a son, and that it would be the seed of the Holy Ghost within her womb. This was after many prophecies of the promise Messiah, Jesus Christ the Lord and King was born.

> *And the angel said unto her, "Fear not, Mary: for you have found favor with God. And Behold' you shall conceive in your womb, and bring forth a son, and shall call His name Jesus.*
> *(Luke 1: 35)*

It was during Israel's celebration of the Feast of Tabernacles that the baby was born in a tent or Sukkot, and the same while the people were thankful to God, they received the gift of the savior. Yet, in John's account he said that Jesus came to His own, but his own knew Him not (John 1:11). In the book of Luke, He states that even though Jesus came as a baby in a cradle, yet His people did not receive Him (Luke 2:9-19).

The Hebrew scholars, in their writings, stated that Jesus was intentionally born to die. His time was limited and His mission was to deliver the message of the Kingdom of God to His people Israel. He accomplished this task as He laid His life down as an atonement for our sins, paying the price for us to be reconciled back to the Father.

Are you curious like I am to know the reason why Jesus came into humanity as a baby? Well, I often wonder why God created Adam and Eve as grownups instead?

God is Intentional

I imagine the reason for babies was to have them receive love and to be taken care of with immediate affection. However, at the beginning of creation the scriptures say that God did not make babies. Is it reasonable to say that He did not want to contend with pampers? I often speculate and question, "Could it be, as the Father of creation, God had lots of things going on and He needed the matured man in order to avoid the baby talk and to get on with His work in adult conversation? God gave the impression when He created Adam and Eve that this was intentional.

It is funny; in my fantasy, I envision that God the Father waited intentionally for Jesus to mature into a teenager. In this stage there would not be any need for pullups. The facts show that Jesus' earthly parents recognized that something had changed with their special son. When Jesus was twelve years old, He had begun to speak like a grownup, and the spirit of God began to lead Jesus into His maturity to do His work (Luke 2:49- 52). At that age, Jesus was heard publicly preaching in the tabernacle. The people thought He displayed an authority. It was His father's business and He was intentionally placed in that position.

The bible declared that Jesus grew and increased in wisdom, statue and in favor with God and man. The priests wondered where Jesus could have acquired His knowledge from. They said that He spoke biblical doctrines. Even His immediate village of Nazareth could not recognize His supernatural ability. They began to categorize Him as the son of Joseph and Mary. Their unbelief caused Jesus to be limited in doing any miracles among them.

The apostle Paul admonished all believers to grow and to mature in the things of God in order to be used of the Lord.

I have deliberated without an answer as to why there are so many leaders in the faith of Jesus Christ who react with such concern when their members have grown and matured out of a state of infancy and into a stage of maturity. The bible has an important point to elaborate on, and that is, that Jesus grew out of His infancy stage, and into a stature of maturity.

This process is called *the theological part of growth and development in a believers' life*. The apostle Paul was beckoning the people not to be stagnant in their faith. He was encouraging them to grow from milk stage into the stage of eating strong meat, where they should study the word for their edification (I Corinthians 3:2-3).

> *For when for the time you ought to be teachers, you have need that one teach you again which be of the oracles of God; and are become such as have need of milk, and not of strong meat.*
> *(Hebrew 5:12-14)*

His Integrity

> *The Lord is not slack concerning His promise, as some men count slackness; but is longsuffering to us-ward, not willing that any should perish, but that all should come to repentance.*
> *(2 Peter 3:9)*

Jesus was authentic throughout His life and ministry. He is the only man with a Divine nature. His trustworthiness was the highlight to Him being a good, good God. He was well-known for His integrity as a truthful and faithful God. Jesus walks in uprightness and perfection, and as God, His morality was of an incorruptible seed. His capability of holiness indicates Jesus was flawless and untarnished.

There were many declarations of His work of deliverances, as He delivered those who were bound and possessed with devils. His creative miracles are showcased as He healed the blind and those who were deaf. In His authority, He performed many miracles of the capacity of feeding the hungry by the thousands. Jesus, in His integrity, had a servant's spirit and humbled himself to wash His disciple feet. In His integrity, He left His divinity and took on humanity. Jesus laid down His life at the Cross. It was love, and He loves you with an eternal love despite your faults.

Go, preach, saying, The Kingdom of heaven is at hand. Heal the sick, cleanse the lepers, raise the dead, cast out devils: freely ye have received, freely give.
(Matthew 10:7-8)

Chapter 11
A TIME FOR DELIVERANCE

The Lord's plan and desire from creation was for us to love and worship Him and do His work. He is looking for the ones with the right attitudes that could capture God's heart. His ultimate desire is to fellowship with you throughout your life and ministry. God intended for man to be infused with fresh encounters and a daily relationship of communion with Him. Jesus has commissioned that all believers will demonstrate God's love and authority, especially in the power of healing and deliverance. His desire is for you to grow and mature in alignment with His word and to have a desire to serve and engage in His work with great confidence. His reassurance for you is that all His promises to you will come to pass for His name sake.

The gift of faith is given to you through the blood of Jesus and those who the evil one tried to possess and take advantage of will be set at liberty. Jesus wants you to serve Him, and in turn, His presence will prevent the devil from gloating about anything concerning you.

The Holy Spirit inspired me to go back and read *Luke 10:18*. I began to review the verses and the following phrase stood out to me: "Jesus said unto them, *'I beheld Satan as lightening fall from heaven.'*" The revelation I received was that Jesus' work was enough; for He has already defeated the enemy.

The devil is a sore loser and this statement should give you confidence that he has no place in your life. These revelations make it exciting as to how you could extend your everyday relationship with the Lord as you seek the application in His word. I pray you will come to a place of knowing that at your command, when you plead the blood of Jesus (in Jesus name), the enemies of your life will fall.

> *And Jesus came and spoke unto them, saying, 'All power is given unto me in heaven and in earth. Go ye therefore, and teach all nations, baptizing them in the name of the Father, and of the Son, and of the Holy Ghost: Teaching them to observe all things whatsoever I have commanded you: and lo, I am with you always, even unto the end of the world. Amen.*
> *(Matthew 28:18-20)*

The Rewards for Obedience

The Lord will give strength to His people to walk in righteousness. There is no righteousness without the Lord. In fact, the scripture says that all our righteousness is like filthy rags (Isaiah 64:6). In the righteousness of God there is complete peace (Psalm 29:11).

In Hebrew the word *"shalom"* means *peace;* it also means *nothing missing*. Other definitions to the word *shalom* signify *a sense of well-being and harmony, both within and without*. This is pertaining to your health, your welfare, and your safety in terms of your completeness or wholeness. The benefits of peace can be determined by the soundness of mind from a state of stress, anxiety and a state of prosperity from the absence of anxiety or discord. This topic of peace will be discussed later in further detail.

In remembrance of the promises of God for our obedience, I will highlight a great story about the prophet Nehemiah. The bible was explicit about how he found peace and strength when doing his task for the Lord. Nehemiah was assigned to conduct the rebuilding the wall of Jerusalem. He began to experience much opposition from the enemies, Tobiah and Sanballat. Although they tried numerous times to stop the construction project, the prophet Nehemiah resisted them by placing his confidence and trust in the God of heaven. He assured the people that God would prosper them to complete the job (Nehemiah 2). I pray that any conspiracy against you will be abolished in the name of Jesus; for the enemy's desire is to fight the plans of the Lord in our lives.

In the book of Acts, the apostle Paul found comfort in Jesus Christ as he obediently went about his journeys to preach the word of the Lord. At times, Paul had experienced various troubles, but he placed his faith and confidence in the Lord Jesus. Paul's confidence kept him encouraged that the Lord had promised to be with him all the way. His ministry has given the believers great courage to do the work of the Lord (Acts 27).

The Consequences of Disobedience

In the kingdom of God there will not be strained relations. God hates the idea of unhealthy relationships. The bible declares that God is not the author of confusion. He is a God that loves and He expects you to walk in love and forgiveness with considerable patience and peace.

"There is no peace to the wicked," says the Lord (Isaiah 48:22). However, in the case of those people who act strange, but are not mentally challenged, God still expects you to also pray for them until God's perfect will is done in their lives. The fact is that when someone is not walking in the light of the Lord, there is a tremendous loss of peace and joy. Their character cannot exercise mercy and grace; truth is also difficult to understand. This is because they find themselves outside the kingdom of God.

The bible declares, 'For we were also once foolish, disobedient, deceiving, serving various lusts and pleasures, living in malice and envy, hateful, and hating one another.' (Titus 3:3)

> 'There is no peace' says the Lord, 'For the wicked.'
> (Isaiah 48:22)

We usually ignore the stories that are told of king Solomon's disobedience that are found in the bible. The story that is often told of king Solomon in the church is surrounding the gifts of discernment he received or the gifts of wisdom and understanding from the Lord. However, Solomon was the first king who turned his heart from God and lead the rebellion to build idolatrous gods. He was instrumental in offering his children to the god of Molech to be burned by the fire as a sacrifice (Kings 11).

The disobedience of king Saul cost him his life and the life of his children. One of the incidents of disobedience that king Saul did was to disobey the Lord and spared the

Amalek king's life. God had told Moses that Amalek was to be destroyed in all their generations (Exodus 17:14). Saul offered up his abominable animals from the tribes for sacrifice to God. God had warned His people not to consult any medium gods. Yet king Saul encouraged the sin and did not expel those who conducted such medium practices. This was his worse sin. In his disobedience, instead of inquiring of the Lord, he inquired of a witch of Endor to practice witchcraft and speak to the prophet Samuel from the dead (1 Samuel 28).

During the disobedience of the children of Israel, the Lord used king Nebuchadnezzar to fulfill His agenda of judgment. He was a heathen king, which tells you that God can use anyone He chooses. After some time, the Lord came to the king and warned him in a dream to change his attitude of pride towards the Hebrew children (Daniel 4). Still, after twelve months, the king did not repent, but set up a golden image of himself and order the people to worship it. The consequences of his pride provoked the judgment of the Lord and Nebuchadnezzar suffered for seven years in the field, eating grass like a beast until he changed his mindset toward God. Afterwards, he was delivered.

This is a lesson for the high-minded and proud. As people of God, we must always remember that no one is better than another person in the Lord's eyes. We discussed in an earlier chapter about the proud look.

God is Holy!

Ye shall be Holy for I the Lord your God am Holy.
(Leviticus 19:2)

Moses had to teach the people the difference between the ways of the 'Righteous' and the ways of the 'Wicked.' According to the commands of the Lord, He had placed a mark of distinction on those He called friends and those He deemed as His enemies.

In order to reflect and mirror His characteristics, the book of Leviticus is a hot topic. I would recommend reading it, because the laws are designed for a holy lifestyle. I read an article from the Hebrew writings and it said that the Hebrew children are taught to read at the age of three years old. This was fascinating to me, that the first bible reading among Hebrew children is the scriptures in the book of Leviticus. They went on to say that the Lord wants His people to understand a series of commandments that He gave concerning the practicality of expressions and the meaning of a daily life of holiness that leads to righteousness.

The Lord requires that His people, who are called by His name, should live a holy and separated life before God. As a believer, it is important to read the Word of God and get an understanding for your life. In order to serve the purposes of God you must permeate yourself with the truth.

Unfortunately, this is the only way that will lead to spiritual blessings. In living, you should be mindful of the experiences that seems to cause the opposite of the blessings to occur. If anyone avoids the principles of truth, it would enable the curses of the Lord to overtake them, in such a way that it warrants a death to spiritual things.

> *There shall in no wise enter into in anything that is defiled, neither whatsoever that work abominations or evil, or make a lie:*

but they which are written in the Lamb's book of life.
(Revelation 21:27)

The Apostle Paul had cautioned Timothy of the foundational things of God. Paul declares that God's word stands sure and it has the seal of Christ's resurrection. He has conveyed to the believers that in the case of them using the name of Christ Jesus, they must depart from iniquity and sins and become holy. In this phrase, Paul continued to say that if you have purged yourself from these wicked things, then you shall become a vessel of honor and will be sanctified and useful for the Father's work (2 Timothy 2:15- 26).

Study to show yourself approved to God, a workman that need not be ashamed, rightly dividing the word of Truth.
(2 Timothy 2:15)

But the servant of the Lord must not strive; but be gentle unto all men, apt to teach, patient, in meekness instructing those that oppose themselves; if God peradventure will give them repentance to the knowledge of the Truth. And that they may recover themselves out of the snare of the devil, who are taken captive by him at his will.
(2 Timothy 2:24-25)

The guarding of your mind is an important thing to cultivate, as it is the doorway to your heart. It is also essential for you to guard your thinking by immersing yourself in the truth. It is better to be grounded in what is truth and real; for it has the tendency to keep your mind stable, so that repentance and mercy will flow freely. As a child of God, you will gain a spiritual understanding. This will cause you to recognize that your identity and your blessings are like a scarce commodity to the Lord.

Peter, the disciple of Jesus Christ, admonished the saints of God to be mindful of the scoffers in these last days. He had warned against the false prophets and the false teachers among them. He reminded the believers of the promise to come and that they are required to be without spots and blameless, and they will dwell in righteousness until the appearing of the new heaven and the new earth.

Peter goes on to warn every believer who knew the truth that they should be aware and be conscious of the schemes of the evil ones in their midst. Beware of those who will lead you away with the error of wickedness and be cautious that you will not fall from your own steadfastness in the faith. These things are flagged alerts, in order that you may grow in grace and in the knowledge of the Lord Jesus Christ. (2 Peter 3). These red signals are seen prevalent in the churches today.

Here is another thing to consider: you should be mindful and take note of what the bible says about God. It says, "In God there is no darkness at all, for God is Light!" It also says that God is Holy and NO unrighteousness is in Him.

If we say we have fellowship with him, and walk in darkness, we lie, and do not the truth: But if we walk in the light, we have fellowship one with another, and the blood of Jesus Christ his Son cleanses us from all sin.
(1 John 1:5-9)

In the writings of Apostle Paul, he had cautioned the saints to become mature in the things of God. He warned us as sheep not to be carried away by all kinds of strange teachings. "Be not carried about with divers and strange doctrines. In order that the believer will to stand firm in their faith, and they be not deceived, as it is a good thing that their hearts be established with grace" (Hebrew 13:9).

As you prevail with the Lord Jesus Christ, your name will be changed. Jacob's repentance produced change and peace within his soul. As you return and repent, you must change your mindset towards the righteousness of the Lord. In the restoration of Jesus Christ, your soul will find peace and you will walk in victory. There will no longer be defeat and disappointments. I read in the bible that your heel will be on the enemy's neck, because Jesus Christ has already bruised his head.

The bible asks the question in Amos 3:3, "Can two walk together, except they be agreed?" The story of Genesis shows us that after a period of time, something went wrong, which brought a disagreement between God and Adam. Adam's sin and disagreement with God caused him to hide himself from God in the garden. God desires to walk with you daily, but like Adam, we find ourselves hiding from the truth. Usually, I find myself getting ahead or falling behind, and the Lord must help me. The Lord God is holy! There is no other God like Him!

Chapter 12
THE BLESSINGS OF GOD

Many people have the perception that God's blessings are basically tangible, material things. They feel that the house they own, the job they have or the car they drive are the blessings of God. The truth is that God's plan for blessing us is that His desires is to place His name on you. He wants to bless you individually and to place upon your life all the blessings of spiritual and physical health, expedient wisdom, knowledge and extravagant prosperity.

There are many principles in the word of God that illustrates that God is Holy. It is obvious that He has shown His determination and desire for the lifestyle of holiness by which He preferences for His people. The Lord will reveal His grace and compassion in your life as you desire to please Him.

The Lord had told Moses to verbally let the priests pronounce blessings over His people. As we look at the priestly blessings, we find that it was first done at Mount Sinai. Aaron, the high priest, was commanded to lift his hands and bless the people at the event. Then the glory of the Lord appeared upon the people where they were gathered (Leviticus 9:22-23). It was important for the Lord's blessings to be on the people, because He desires to put His name on them.

In His nature of love and compassion, the Lord shown in His actions that He had taken into consideration the fear factor of the people. It was difficult to take the step of faith, not knowing where they were going; and this was highlighted in their action of a rebellious nature. They needed the assurance that the Lord will be with them; for the children of Israel were venturing into an unknown territory, and at this time they needed strength, power and wisdom for their journey into the Promise Land.

According to the scriptures, on the last day before Jesus ascended into heaven, He blessed His disciples. This was the last act of His love upon the earth. The Hebrew scholars say that customarily the people would bow their heads and look down to the earth in reverence to God. They would not look directly into the priest's face, because it was said that it would be a distraction to him. Therefore, as Jesus raised His nailed scarred hands to bless them, they bowed their heads in reverence. Their eyes were looking downward to His nailed scarred feet and they saw His feet raising off the ground. When Jesus concluded the blessing, He had ascended into the clouds and that was the reason why the disciples looked up and began gazing into heaven. Then the angel appeared and inquired of the disciples what they were gazing at. He told them that the same way Jesus departed is the same way He would return one day.

In Luke's version, he mentioned that Jesus led them out as far as Bethany, then lifted up His hands and blessed them (Luke 24:50). This revealed that Jesus in His priestly office was putting His name upon them.

During the rulership of king David, he encouraged all the congregation to bless the Lord God. Therefore, all the congregation of Israel blessed the Lord God of their fathers, bowed down their heads, and worshipped their Lord and their king (1 Chronicles 29:20). Their actions convey the stance and attitude necessary for praises and blessings to the Lord for His goodness towards you.

> *Blessed be the God and Father of our Lord Jesus Christ, who had blessed us with all spiritual blessings in heavenly place in Christ.*
> *(Ephesians 1:3)*

> *"I will cause the shower to come down in his season; there shall be showers of blessings," says the Lord.*
> *(Ezekiel 34:26)*

I have good news today. The Lord is determined to bless you, and in blessing you, He will place His name as an identity upon your life. In the book of Numbers, chapter six, it has depicted that the prayer of blessings will grow into intensity. The sages say that the Lord's blessings will replicate like the waves of a Tsunami.

According to the apostle Paul, the blessings of God are in the fullness of the gospel of Christ (Romans 15:29). In fact, the blessings of the Lord will come to you repeatedly, and it drowns you. The word *drown* means *to submerge or engulf you with His blessings*. The psalmist went on to say that the Lord in His compassion will uphold all those that fall and raise up all those that are bowed down, in the name of Jesus (Psalm 145:14).

The Aaronic Blessing

Hebrew scholars, in their commentary, say that the Aaronic Blessing was separated into three parts. The first three words are the *"Lord Bless You!"* and the second five words say, *"And the Lord keep you."* The next verse says, *"The Lord lifts up His countenance upon you* (or to make His face to shine upon you!) *and give you peace."*

Their explanation of the Aaronic Blessing of Numbers 6:24-27 has formed an expansion to my understanding of God's promise to His people. Their analogy is that there are fifteen (15) Hebrew letters in the first verse, twenty (20) letters in the second verse and twenty-five (25) in the last verse. The total amount of letters is equivalent to sixty (60). Therefore, the Hebrew numeric value and the concept of the blessing was in relevance to the meaning of "the arms of a man lifted." They went to say that there are thirty bones in each arm and this is equivalent to sixty bones in two arms. This scientific concept is in comparison to the High Priest lifting his hands to bless the people.

It is only God that can articulate such a creative concept in our life. It shows that the blessings of the Lord should be resolute in your life. You will reflect the Lord in your looks. Moreover, the book of Psalms reveals that the posture for the blessing is to be on bending knees. This is the primary way to bless and worship our Lord God (Psalm 95:6).

In the family arena, the Lord's desire for the father is to speak this Aaronic blessing over his family. Also, the husband should say this blessing over his wife. However, in the case of the absence of the father figure in your life, then a spiritual father should say this blessing over you. And the Lord instructed the priest to say:

The Lord Bless you, and keep you:
The Lord makes His face shine upon you:

The Blessings of God

*The Lord lift up His countenance upon you,
and give you peace. (Shalom)
(Numbers 6:24-26)*

1. The Lord Bless You!

In the New Testament, Jesus came on bended knees as He humbly gave His life as the greatest blessing at the cross at Calvary. The Lord desires to come and bless you with eternal life. To put His action in perspective, I would like to say that Jesus took on the form of a slave, humble himself to the cross, to bless you and your family.

> *Jesus made himself of no reputation, and took upon Him the form of a servant, and was made in the likeness of me: And being found in fashion as a man, He humbled himself, and became obedient unto death, even the death of the cross.*
> *(Philippians 2:7-8)*

2. The Lord keep you!

The Hebrew word for 'keep' is *Shamar*. It also means *to watch and to protect*. Jesus wants to place a hedge around you with thorns from every predator of your life – the way a shepherd usually builds a hedge around the flock and guard and protect them from predators. This illustration is seen in the nature of the shepherd and his flock of sheep in the Hebrew culture in Israel.

> *Now unto Him that is able to keep you from falling, and to present you faultless before the presence of His glory with exceeding joy, to the only wise God our*

*Savior, be glory and majesty, dominion and power,
both now and forever. Amen*
(Jude 1:24-25)

3.   The Lord lift up His face to shine on you!
The word for *'shine'* means *as the beam of light.* God wants to look at you directly in your eyes, eyeball-to-eyeball, and face-to-face. He wants to lift your face up if you have sinned and it will cause you to bend your head down. The Lord's face is like light and it will be shining on you, in your heart and in your soul (2 Corinthians 4:6). As a believer, when you have the word of God in your life it is a light; it will shine the light and like a reflecting mirror, His knowledge and understanding will reveal truth.

However, if there is the case of sin, and it is still operating in your life, the light of His countenance will become dim, and this will eventually cause the Lord to hide His face from you (Genesis 1:16-17).

4.   The Lord be gracious to you!
God's grace includes three levels of *'Mercy'* which we will take a look at. One of God's names is Gracious, and Merciful Kindness. The first level of grace is that which He extends to all humans, and it is shed abroad in everyone's heart. The second level is His targeted blessings. This is where the Lord personally gets involve in your life. And the third level of grace causes Him to lift your head up so that you can look into His eyes.

These are quotes from the bible, and the sages say that it is like the father who lifts his child to his eye level and smiles at that child. As the Lord lifts your head, you will be able to look into His eyes (Psalm 31:9).

The Blessings of God

His merciful kindness is great towards everybody. (Psalm 117:2) He gives mercy to you! He will declare His name before you, wherever you go (Exodus 33:19). God will adopt you like a parent or like the mother with a baby in her womb. In the same way, Jesus will come down and be involved in your life. The bible declares, "While we were yet sinners; Christ died for us" (Roman 5:8).

> *Having predestined us unto the adoption of children of Jesus Christ Himself, according to the good pleasure of His will. To the praise and glory of His grace.*
> *(Ephesians 1:5-7)*

5.   The Lord lift up His countenance upon you!
You should not let your face be hung down in the posture of shame and guilt. In your repentance, you will be restored and be sanctified by the blood of Jesus and His truth. The Lord desires to really shine in you, that the radiance of His Love will shine through you and extend to others. This process will take time and will include rectification to your spirit man.

6.   The Lord will give you peace!
Peace in Hebrew language is the word 'Shalom.' The Lord Jesus will look into your eyes, as He loves to smile at you. He will guard your heart and restore and protect your soul. There will be a rejuvenated state of an internal peace; the kind of peace that only the Lord can give. (John 16:7) The bible says that peace flows like a river in the soul, there will be nothing missing.

The peace of God, which pass all understanding, shall keep your hearts and minds through Christ.
(Philippians 4:7)

So let us come boldly to the throne of our gracious God. There we will receive His mercy, and we will find grace to help us when we need it most
(Hebrew 4:16)

All Praise to Adonai!

King David recognized that the blessings of the Lord were practices of life by faith. He had multiple experiences of failure, but he also had several pleasant victories in his life. As a result of these experiences, he ascribed his thanksgiving to God into many songs as we see in the book of Psalms. These Psalms are quoted as a part of the believers' prayer life. Today, they are still sung in times of trouble and despair. David was encouraged to praise the Lord in every situation of life, regardless of how it seems.

David had declared that the Lord is great in mercies and quick to pardon our sins. However, as a reminder, the Lord forgives unintentional sins, but not our deliberate sins. In fact, you should strive to desire His help in every area of our life. The scriptures say that out of His love for humanity, Jesus gave His life on the Cross in humility. He was sacrificed as the Lamb of God to buy back our salvation and to redeem and restore our peace.

> *The Lamb which is in the midst of the throne shall feed them, and shall lead them unto living fountains of waters: and God shall wipe away all tears from their eyes.*
> (Revelation 7:17)

His Kingdom is Full of Love

Throughout the bible, the Lord's justice and judgment is final. In the Book of Galatians, it summarizes the law in one phrase, "Love yourself, and love others."

Jesus declares that in His kingdom in Heaven there is an abundance of love. Therefore, the only currency available in His kingdom is **Love.** You might ask the question, "Why love ?" The answer is clearly seen that the Love factor is the first and second command from God's perspective (Deuteronomy 6:4-5).

The definition for *what true love is* in the Hebraic language conveys the meaning, *"it is simply to obey and do."* In one of Jesus' meetings, He said, "You shall love God and love your neighbor as yourself" (Mark 12:31).

> *For the whole law is fulfilled in one word, in this: "You shall love your neighbor as yourself." But if you bite and devour one another, be careful that you don't consume one another. But I say, walk by the Spirit, and you won't fulfill the lust of the flesh.*
> (Galatians 5:14-16)

The phrase that rings true to me is the definition that Apostle John used to define *"what love is not."* He was in fact accurate and very explicit to the teaching at that time of the Lord Jesus (1 John 4:12).

> *No man hath seen God at any time. If we love one another, God dwells in us, and his love is perfected in us.*
> *(1 John 4:12)*

> *If a man says, I love God, and hate his brother, he is a liar: for He that love not his brother whom he hath seen, how can he love God whom he hath not seen?*
> *(1 John 4:20)*

One important factor in the kingdom of God is to walk upright in order to live in righteousness and love. David, in the book of Psalms, gave a few examples of someone walking in uprightness with the Lord.

> *"He that walk uprightly, work righteousness, and speak the truth in his heart. He that backbite not with his tongue, nor do evil to his neighbor, nor take up a reproach against his neighbor."*
> *(Psalms 15:2-3)*

The principles of the righteous man are:

1. Walking in right standing with the Lord.
2. Work in the decency of the morals of life.
3. Speak honestly in your heart.

4. Never cultivate habits of spitefulness and badmouthing.
5. Never do mischief to your neighbor.
6. Never take up an accusation against your neighbor.

> *Mark the perfect man, and behold the upright, for the end of that man is peace.*
> *(Palms 37:37)*

> The problem is not the Law. For it is written, "Who is wise? He shall understand these things" (Hosea 14:9).

Here is a great illustration of choosing Jesus Christ. It is the story between Jesus and the woman at the well. The description of the state of the Samaritan woman was that all her life she had felt rejected. In her case, she was being rejected by her family, and she found herself in the predicament of barrenness in her marriages. Her dilemma caused the ladies to gossip about her. Besides, she was born a Samaritan and the Jews had a rejection toward her. Therefore, she thought that Jesus, being a Jew, would not accept her.

Instead, Jesus told her of the salvation plan, and in His compassion, explained that if she desired to know the Lord of Abraham, it will be her choice. Jesus simply revealed that if she would believe with her whole heart and allow the Holy Spirit to reveal Christ to her, she would not be rejected by the Savior. There was evidence that showed how she had allowed herself to believe in what other people said about Christ the Redeemer. The choice was now hers to believe that Jesus was Lord and Redeemer. In doing so, she had received the revelation of her salvation.

History has revealed a testimony that the Samaritan woman's life was changed forever and her ministry began when she won the whole village to Jesus Christ.

The hour has come, and now is, when the true worshippers shall worship the Father in spirit and in truth: for the Father seeks such to worship Him.
(John 4:23-24)

God's Authority is Final!

If the Lord should mark iniquities, O Lord who shall stand? But there is forgiveness with You. That You may be feared.
(Psalms 130: 3-4)

In Proverbs, the writer told the son to keep his father's commandments and not to forsake his mother's law: but he should keep it in his heart and tie it like a necklace around his neck (Proverbs 6:23). The bible says that: "You shall serve the Lord your God, and He will bless your bread and water, and take away sickness from among you (Exodus 23:25-27).

The Lord shall endure forever: He had prepared His throne for judgment. He shall judge the world in righteousness.
(Psalm 9:7-8)

The books are open…………...

Forever O Lord Your Word is settled in Heaven
(Psalms 119:89)

My prayer for you, today!

May the Lord Jesus Christ help you and take away the veil from over your eyes, that you may see the things of God, and not only things of this world. May the Lord take away all the darkness from around you.

    I pray that your heart be receptive to the love of the Father God and His son Jesus Christ.

    I pray that you will let your light shine towards others, that they may be drawn to see a radiant path towards the Lord Jesus (Ephesian 1:18-19).

May the Lord open your heart to respond to His love for His laws.

    May your length of days be as your desire for the truth, for you to diligently keep all the commands of the Lord like a garland upon your neck.

Amen.

About the Author

Wynette A. Tyrrell is a teacher of the word of God. Her ministry is unique to an audience of all ages. Her passion is to equip other believers to specifically understand the gospel with truth and simplicity.

Wynette loves to see people transformed by the knowledge of the power of God. Her writing is a highlight to the overlooked principles of the Word of God that are enlightening, but ordinarily read. Her message is the spiritual insight of revelations concerning the Justice and Judgment of God.

She is dedicated to family, and her devotion to love people is exceptional and empathetic.

In a sequel to the truth of the Justice and Judgment of God, she has written a book entitled, "Look What Jesus Did!"

Look What Jesus Did!
ISBN: 978-1-947741-13-3